Green Roof Plants

Green Roof Plants

A Resource and Planting Guide

Edmund C. Snodgrass
Lucie L. Snodgrass

TIMBER PRESS

Frontispiece: *Talinum* and mixed sedums on a test roof at
Emory Knoll Farms in Street, Maryland.

Published in 2006 by
Timber Press, Inc.
The Haseltine Building
133 S.W. Second Avenue, Suite 450
Portland, Oregon 97204-3527, U.S.A.
www.timberpress.com
For contact information regarding editorial, marketing, sales, and
distribution in the United Kingdom, see www.timberpress.co.uk.

Printed in Hong Kong

Library of Congress Cataloging-in-Publication Data

Snodgrass, Edmund C.
   Green roof plants : a resource and planting guide / Edmund C.Snodgrass
and Lucie L. Snodgrass.
       p. cm.
   Includes bibliographical references and index.
     ISBN-13: 978-0-88192-787-0
     ISBN-10: 0-88192-787-2
  1. Green roofs (Gardening) 2. Landscape plants. 3. Ground cover plants.
  I. Snodgrass, Lucie L. II. Title.
     SB419.5.S66 2006
     635.9'671—dc22

                                                2006013821

A catalog record for this book is also available from the British Library.

To Dr. David Beattie, whose wit is surpassed only by his knowledge, and to Dr. John White, whose generosity and erudition made this book possible.

Together, these men have made valuable contributions to the world of horticulture, culminating in the emerging field of green roofs.

Contents

Acknowledgments

IN AN INDUSTRY so young, it is easy to remember the beginnings and the people who introduced me to green roofs. Katrin Scholz-Barth first told me that my plants had a home of which they were unaware. Dale Hendricks, connector extraordinaire, introduced me to David Beattie at Penn State, and Dr. Beattie and I traveled to Ottawa to a small green roof conference organized by Steven Peck of Green Roofs for Healthy Cities. Charlie Miller, Matt Carr, and Mark Gaulin all became pioneers in promoting green roofs in my area of the United States.

Thanks to Kurt Bluemel for my introduction to horticulture, and also to Georg Uebelhart, a young Swiss intern when I first met him and now a world-class plantsman and dear friend. Georg was instrumental in helping with the plant list for this book. Big thanks go to Panayoti Kelaidis from the Denver Botanic Gardens for his generosity of time, information, and spirit in building the plant list.

Thanks are due to the academics who kept this farm boy in line: Dr. Bill Hunt at North Carolina State, Dr. Brad Rowe at Michigan State, and Drs. David Beattie, Robert Berghage, and John White (emeritus) of Penn State.

Larry Reed of SWA Group, Sarah Wayland-Smith of Balmori, and Brooke Whiting Cash of Richard Burck Associates were great collaborative people who taught me a lot about how to interface with the worlds of architects and landscape architects. Thanks to Jörg Breuning and Peter Philippi for sharing their expertise and decades of experience on German green roofs, and to Bob and Richard Saul, two visionaries and one of my favorite sets of brothers.

Special thanks to my business partner, John Shepley, and to the staff at Emory Knoll Farms for all their support, and to Sarah Murphy for taking on a summer internship focused on plant research for this book.

Finally, thanks to my family: my sons, Graham and Tim, for their support; my wife, Lucie, for all the writing and editing; and my parents, Tom and Oleta Snodgrass, for giving me the incomparable experience of growing up on a farm, and their unconditional love and support throughout my life.

EDMUND C. SNODGRASS

WRITING THIS BOOK would not have been possible without the help of the experts who coached me throughout. First and foremost is Dr. John White, professor emeritus of horticulture at Penn State, who generously shared his vast knowledge of horticulture and green roofs and agreed to help me in any way possible with this endeavor, just so it would see the light of day. That included reading, correcting, and adding substantially to whatever materials I sent him. Thank you, also, to Peggy White, who was a wonderful hostess on a visit to her and John's beautiful home and garden in Colorado. The book also owes much to Drs. David Beattie and Robert Berghage of Penn State; Dr. Bradley Rowe of Michigan State; Dr. Bill Hunt of North Carolina State; Mark Gaulin of Magco, Inc.; Jörg Breuning of Green Roof Service; and Charlie Miller of Roofscapes, Inc., all of whom read, commented on, and greatly improved the book at various stages. Thank you from the bottom of my heart to John Shepley, whose genius on the computer and calm demeanor were my saving grace.

I am also grateful to Tom Fischer, Joe Kuffner, and Eve Goodman, our editors at Timber Press, for their guidance, wisdom, and support throughout this project, and to Lisa Theobald, for all her expertise and patience.

Special thanks go to my sister, Alexandra, who is always there for me and learned more about green roofs than she ever wanted to, and to Joann Blewett, Nancy Talbot, and Catherine Fox, three of the most supportive friends I could ever ask for.

LUCIE L. SNODGRASS

Introduction

TEN YEARS PRIOR to this book's release, a plant guide for green roofs would not have found a market in the United States. Even five years previously, the idea would have been premature. While the concept of planting roofs has long been championed and practiced in Germany and is increasingly common in Japan, as well as Switzerland, Austria, and other northern European countries, it is still in its infancy in the United States. In recent years, however, growing concerns about the environmental and economic costs of development have done a great deal to open minds to the concept of green roofs in North America. From the unappealing aesthetics of acres of flat roofs, to the growing negative impact of the urban heat island effect, to pollution caused by unrestrained water runoff, many compelling reasons prompt us to seek out more innovative approaches to managing problems and challenges associated with development. And whereas a decade ago finding even a single extensive green roof in North America would have been a rarity, today hundreds, moving into thousands, of successful installations can be found around the United States and Canada, ranging from private homes, to universities and colleges, to large corporations such as Gap, Inc., and the Ford Motor Company. And increasingly, federal agencies and institutions in the United States, including the Department of Defense, the National Institutes of Health, and the Library of Congress, are also sporting green roofs.

Interest in green roofs is coming from myriad fronts, leading to incremental changes in public and environmental policy and shifts in site and building designs, and a new awareness of the role green roofs can play—from improving the look of the developed landscape, to mitigating the harmful effects of storm water runoff on major bodies of water such as the Chesapeake Bay, as well as countless rivers, streams, and aquifers.

As any market develops and matures, services follow, and this is gradually occurring in the green roof industry. Architects, engineers, roofers, landscape designers and installers, among others, are starting to tailor their skills, services, and products to clients in this emerging field. European suppliers are rapidly entering the North American market, which has already led to an expansion of products available here. More products are entering the market every year. Equally important, groundbreaking research on green roofs is underway at Penn State University, North Carolina State University, and Michigan State University, including trials on how medium content and depth affect plant growth and how well green roofs retain and detain water. The emerging data are invaluable in advancing specific knowledge of green roof systems in North America and in predicting their future successes. Increasingly, too, green roofs are the subject of national and international conferences, thanks in part to two advocacy organizations: New York–based Earth Pledge and Toronto's Green Roofs for Healthy Cities. Green roofs are also beginning to impact public policy in such cities as Toronto, Chicago, and Portland, Oregon, providing economic incentives—including tax breaks—to encourage green roofs on new and retrofitted buildings.

Even with all the recent activity, however, reliable information about green roofs had been difficult to find in English, apart from conference proceedings. In part this was because no long-lived extensive green roofs exist in North America, but the American market was also hampered by the fact that most of the authoritative texts were available only in German. That changed with the 2004 publication of Nigel Dunnett and Nöel Kingsbury's book *Planting Green Roofs and Living Walls* (Timber Press 2004), which offers an excellent overview of the subject in English and addresses all aspects of green roofs, ranging from design and engineering specifications to installation and maintenance.

This book focuses more narrowly on green roof plants and attempts to offer specific guidance on what plants are most likely to succeed on extensive green roofs in a variety of conditions and settings across North America. It is a daunting task, and inevitably we will not do it perfectly. Because climatic conditions across North America vary dramatically from northern Europe, where the majority of green roofs are installed, past efforts to adapt plant specifications from Germany, where the climate is milder and more predictably moist, have been largely unsuccessful. North America's wide range of weather patterns that extend from one extreme to another, combined with the nascent stage of the green roof market here, make it likely that experimentation and failure will go hand in hand for the foreseeable future. This is especially true for such areas as the southwestern United States, where virtually no extensive green roofs exist—irrigated or not. While it is possible to extrapolate some of what has been learned in Europe, other knowledge, including that about medium composition and depth and plant tolerance to extreme weather conditions, can be gained only through practical experience here.

This book is written for a general audience that includes gardeners, environmental activists, and ecologically minded do-it-yourself homeowners, but it is targeted specifically at professionals involved in the emerging green roof industry—landscape designers and installers, engineers, roofers, and architects, in particular. It is not aimed at horticultural experts, although some aspects of the book may be of interest to them insofar as it pertains to adaptive uses of plants. The book aims to offer reliable and detailed plant options suitable for a wide range of extensive green roof projects throughout North America. This applies for USDA hardiness zones 2 through 9, sheltered and exposed locations, and sunny and shaded spots. Included in the options are xeric plants, some herbaceous perennials and natives, and grasses and annuals, although the majority of the recommended plants are drought-hardy succulents, especially *Sedum* and *Delosperma* species. Thus, we hope that design professionals working on separate green roofs in New York, Toronto, and Los Angeles will all be able to consult the book and meet their varying project and design needs.

Still, it must be noted that green roofs are still so new to North America that no tried-and-true plant lists exist for use here. Hence, it is impossible to offer fail-proof plant lists, as might be possible in other landscaping contexts. Inevitably, as the market becomes more established, certain plants deemed suitable for some sites will not work as well as intended, whereas other plants that might not have been considered initially will turn out to work very well. In addition, since most green roofs are primarily functional in nature, we are sure to find systems that are optimized by plants that are more functional than aesthetic, or that are governed by different goals for a particular green roof. Therefore, plant specifications are relative to function, and plant lists can and will change for reasons other than site considerations.

For readers who may not be familiar with certain aspects of green roofs, the book offers practical information on green roof assembly as well as short sections on green roof site design, installation, and maintenance. The bulk of the book, however, is devoted to the plants themselves, a compendium of more than 200 plants suitable for application on extensive green roofs, with detailed information about what works best where and under what conditions. It is organized alphabetically by genus, and an appendix listing plants by their characteristics is also provided. We provide as much information as possible about each plant, its genus and species, and its attributes, including hardiness characteristics, light requirements, bloom time and color, and whether it is best utilized as a groundcover or an accent plant. In addition, we provide information about general characteristics, such as whether plants are self sowing. Finally, the book lists experienced green roof seed and plant suppliers. All of this is included to provide as much relevant information as possible, so that readers can make intelligent choices about plant selection for green roof projects.

CHAPTER 1

Green Roof Fundamentals

T HE IDEA OF GREENING A ROOF dates back thousands of years. Civilizations in Mesopotamia originated the concept (Dunnett and Kingsbury 2004), and Greeks, Romans, Persians, and other cultures had some form of roof gardens to green and cool their often brutally hot landscapes. The famed Hanging Gardens of Babylon, for example, were actually planted on rooftops. At the other climatic extreme, sod roofs have long graced homes in Scandinavia, providing extra warmth and insulation in cold, wet climates. Nature itself is the inspiration for green roofs, as self-sown seeds germinate in leaf, dirt, and rock piles on garden sheds, in gutters, and on seemingly inhospitable, often flat, stretches of roof.

Green roofs did not attain widespread use until more recent times, and then only in parts of northern Europe, where the scarcity of land for new buildings, combined with the development of new roofing materials such as concrete, were driving forces behind their modern adaptation. When Switzerland, Germany, Austria, and other countries embarked on a post–World War II building campaign, builders utilized green roofs for practical, environmental, and aesthetic purposes. As cities expanded to the edges of the countryside, green roofs represented an innovative way to preserve green space, reduce the impact of development, and help filter and purify the air. Planted roofs increased oxygen output, softened urban streetscapes, reduced impervious surfaces, and contained storm water runoff to vital tributaries and major bodies of water that supplied drinking water to millions of people.

Germany has emerged as the world leader not only in developing green roof technologies and systems, but in passing federal and state legislation to mandate green roofs under specific conditions and offering economic incentives to install them. The state of Nordrhein-Westfalen, for example, pays individuals who install green roofs €15.00 per square meter (Herman 2003), while other states offer similar programs.

The Germans are also responsible for developing detailed guidelines for green roof planning and installation through the Forschungsgesellschaft Landschaftsentwicklung Landschaftsbau (FLL), or Landscape Research,

A replica of an early sod house in Iceland.

A modern chalet in Switzerland features a green roof that mimics its surroundings.

Germany's stringent regulations governing new development make green roofs a common sight throughout German cities, as this view of Stuttgart shows.

Development and Construction Society. So accepted is the concept of greening roofs in Germany that by 2001, approximately 14 percent of all German flat roofs, or more than 145 million square feet (13.5 million square meters), had been greened (Herman 2003). In neighboring Switzerland, 12 percent of flat roofs are green, and both Swiss and German federal laws state that development must avoid unnecessary disturbances to the environment and that developers must compensate for any displacement of open space. Switzerland further requires that 25 percent of new commercial development must be greened.

Green roofs are planted for a wide variety of reasons and with different goals in mind—from sheer aesthetic pleasure to storm water runoff management, climate cooling, water filtration, food production, and habitat restoration. But any green roof, whether a simple mat of sedums or an elaborately varied ecosystem such as the roof that graces Chicago's City Hall, has a net positive impact on its surroundings. A well-designed and planted green roof not only pleases the eye, it potentially doubles the life of the roof; attenuates sound inside a building; lowers indoor and outdoor ambient temperatures in summer, thus saving energy costs; and absorbs and filters impurities in the air. A green roof acts, in ecologists Nancy and John Todd's words, as a "living machine" to retain water and reduce harmful runoff (Todd 1993). And best of all, green roofs perform these functions simultaneously.

Extensive green roofs, or vegetated roofs that typically comprise less than 6 in. (15 cm) of mostly inorganic substrate, were an anomaly in North America until around the year 2000. When they existed at all, they were found on private homes or the occasional office building and garnered a good bit of curiosity and even skepticism. *Intensive* roofs, which employ a much deeper, more organic substrate and rely on irrigation systems to re-create full-scale gardens above the ground, were more common. Still, on a continent with vast areas of open space, even intensive roofs have not achieved widespread use, except in densely populated urban areas.

Since the beginning of the new century, however, the governments of both Canada and the United States have begun to embrace the European model of green roofs and adopt progressive building standards and protocols that encourage and reward environmentally sustainable practices, including green roofs. In 2004, for example, the Canadian government began including green roofs in a continuum of sustainable initiatives eligible for partial

The green roof on this residential home in Maryland not only beautifies its surroundings, it also reduces storm water runoff into the Severn River, a major tributary of the Chesapeake Bay.

reimbursement and funding (Peck 2005). This encouraged a surge of green roof activity, especially in Toronto, which, like Chicago, planted the roof on its city hall. In the United States, the General Services Administration and Department of Defense now mandate that all of their new buildings adhere to green building protocols developed by the US Green Building Council, which includes green roofs as one method of achieving a higher environmental rating under the Leadership in Energy and Environmental Design (LEED) initiative. And Regions 1, 2, and 8 of the US Environmental Protection Agency (EPA) are exploring green roofs on some of their buildings. Several US states, among them Oregon, Maryland, and California, have begun offering tax incen-

A plaque denotes that this building has achieved a gold rating from the US Green Building Council's Leadership in Energy and Environmental Design (LEED) initiative.

Intensive green roofs similar to this one on the Grove Park Inn in Ashville, North Carolina, are much more common than extensive green roofs in North America.

tives for incorporating green building practices into the design and construction of new government and commercial buildings.

Not surprisingly, much of the North American impetus for green roofs stems from urban areas such as Toronto, Chicago, and Portland, Oregon. In these cities, greens roofs offer a practical means of achieving financial savings in energy and water treatment costs, while also effecting better environmental conditions for their residents.

Now that 1.5 percent of the lower 48 United States is covered by impervious surfaces—an area roughly the size of Ohio and growing (Elvidge et al. 2004)—problems associated with urban and suburban sprawl are on the increase and cannot be ignored. Chief among them are a decrease in water quality; the inability of water to reach and replenish aquifers; storm water overwhelming the very systems that are designed to carry it away; more radiant surfaces, causing the urban heat island effect (in which a combination of structural and pavement heat fluxes and pollutants form "islands" of elevated temperatures); an increase in low-level ozone readings; and a surfeit of particulate matter in the air. Deaths associated with the urban heat island effect are on the rise, and it is estimated that by the year 2050, a 253 percent in-

Unplanted black roofs contribute to a rise in ambient temperature and are still the norm in many North American cities, such as Baltimore.

crease in heat-related summer mortality will be realized (New York Climate and Health Project 2004).

Green Roof Benefits

Green roofs, while not panaceas, offer measurable benefits. They are most valuable in the mitigation and even elimination of water runoff problems associated with growth and development. Current research underway at North Carolina State University in storm water management suggests, for example, that green roofs with 4 in. (10 cm) of substrate retain as much as 60 percent of all rainwater, which has tremendous potential for addressing storm water runoff and water quality (Moran et al. 2005). And green roofs, unlike other tools that address discrete environmental goals or problems, accomplish multiple goals simultaneously. So, while detention ponds, another tool used to contain storm water runoff, are effective at doing that, unless they are vegetated, they do not filter particulate matter or improve water quality, as green roofs can.

Green roof trials at North Carolina State University's JC Raulston Arboretum in Raleigh.

Green roofs and other vegetated areas also offer simultaneous aesthetic and practical benefits. Planting areas otherwise lost to development softens and greens the surroundings, drawing attention to something other than asphalt or other impervious surfaces, especially in urban settings. But vegetation does more: it provides habitat for birds and insects, sequesters carbon dioxide and other pollutants, purifies the air, produces oxygen, and returns moisture and coolness to the air through evapotranspiration. In Europe, where populations are more densely concentrated than in North America, intensive and extensive green roofs are also frequently designed as recreational or open spaces, including plazas and playgrounds over underground parking garages. In England, so-called "eco roofs" are specifically designed to provide habitat in highly populated areas for bird species such as black redstarts (*Phoenicurus ochruros*) (Gedge 2003).

Green roofs, among other environmentally beneficial practices in and on buildings, also have a positive impact on the people living or working around them. This is borne out by a 2003 report showing worker productivity in green buildings to be substantially higher than in buildings that are less environmentally friendly (Kats 2004). That same study shows that green building practices, contrary to expectations, can also be cost effective in the long run, despite higher upfront costs, because of savings accrued in measurable areas, including declining worker absenteeism and electricity usage. Consider, for example, the mixed intensive and extensive green roof that Chicago installed on its City Hall in 2001. The ambient summer temperature on the roof is roughly equivalent to the outside ambient temperature. By contrast, typical black asphalt roofs regularly experience temperatures twice that of the atmospheric temperature, with readings as high as 175°F (79°C). The cooling effect is achieved in several ways: through shading, evapotranspiration, and increased insulation of the building. Research on urban heat island mitigation conducted by scientists at the Lawrence Berkeley National Laboratory in Berkeley, California, shows that cooler roofs—those painted white or planted—reduce annual air conditioning costs by tens of mil-

A killdeer nests on a green roof just outside Washington, D.C.

lions of dollars in jurisdictions that have implemented heat island mitigation measures. If more roofs were greened, national energy savings could be in the billions of dollars (Pomerantz et al. 1999).

According to data from Green Roofs for Healthy Cities (2004), up to 75 percent of many cities are covered in impervious surfaces, and roofs account for a large part of these. Roofs in the Canadian city of Toronto make up between 15 and 30 percent of total impervious surfaces. In Portland, Oregon, alone, roofs account for 25 square miles of city surface. It is easy to see how roofs are both a part of the current problems associated with urban heat island effects and storm water runoff, but they could also be part of the potential solution. The rapid disappearance of open land has increased the amount of impervious surfaces, exacerbating runoff problems by reducing the amount of ground surface available to absorb water. The problem is most acute in US cities where aging storm and sewer systems are partially or wholly combined, which occurs frequently. When a heavy downpour and sewage converge in the same waste stream for treatment, a facility's ability to contain and treat the combined sewer overflow (CSO) is quickly overwhelmed, forcing the release of untreated or partially treated sewage directly into rivers, bays, and other open bodies of water. In 2003, for example, the

Studies have shown that a view from an office onto a green roof can contribute to higher worker productivity and a sense of well being on the part of the building's occupants.

city of Washington, D.C., which has 59 combined sewer outfalls, resorted to dumping more than 3 billion gallons of raw sewage annually into Rock Creek and the Anacostia and Potomac rivers (Earth Justice 2004). The discharges regularly led to violations of environmental standards for bacteria, oxygen, and other pollutants, and resulted in a consortium of environmental groups filing suit (and winning) against the Washington Area Sewer Authority (WASA) to force it to reduce instances of CSO and develop a better plan for handling it.

In 1990, solutions for dealing with runoff were limited and extremely costly: either expand the diameter of the storm water and sewage pipes or add more sewage treatment capacity. Today, however, more sustainable solutions such as detention ponds, rain gardens, vegetated swales, and especially green roofs offer alternatives. If impervious surfaces indeed make up as much as 75 percent of urban areas, then 75 percent of a normal rain is not being absorbed into the ground and aquifers, but instead runs off into city storm or sewer drains. When that same area is planted with a green roof, however, up to 90 percent of that storm water is captured, and the water that eventually runs off does so over periods of hours and days rather than minutes, allowing for gradual absorption into the ground. A 4 in. (10 cm) extensive green roof system, for example, sequesters on average about 60 percent of annual rainfall, and even a 2 in. (5 cm) substrate will retain roughly 50 per-

A green roof was planted on the Earth Conservation Corps building overlooking the Anacostia River in Washington, D.C., as part of a settlement agreement to reduce instances of raw sewage overflow.

A green roof on the Boston World Trade Center helps to reduce storm water runoff into Boston Harbor.

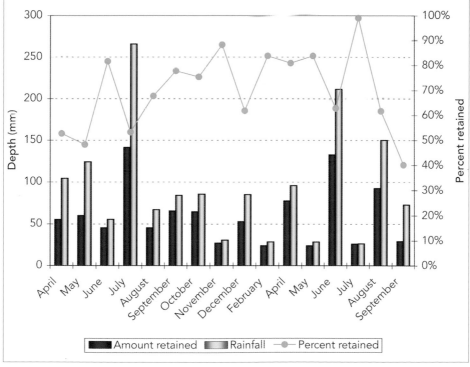

Wayne Community College green roof retention (April 2003–September 2004).
Courtesy of North Carolina State University.

cent of a ½-inch rainfall in a storm. Results from a test site administered by North Carolina State at Wayne Community College in Goldsboro, North Carolina, showed that a 2 in. (5 cm) green roof reduced by half the runoff that would otherwise end up in storm or sewer drains (Hunt 2005).

Green roofs, depending on the composition and depth of their medium, can also play critical roles in purifying water and air by absorbing nitrogen and remediating the acidity of the water running off of the roofs. As part of the landmark decision in the lawsuit filed against WASA, the sewer authority agreed to fund $2 million in greening projects, including green roofs, along the Anacostia River (Earth Justice 2004). The greening was targeted at retaining and purifying water entering the watershed and reducing runoff and pollution.

Obviously, green roofs alone cannot solve environmental problems resulting from development. In North America, where green roofs are still a novelty, it will take years to measure, quantify, and publicize the full benefits that accrue as a result of them. Increasingly, however, public policy makers, builders, and others are realizing that green roofs are a part of a greening strategy for cities and suburban areas, without which it becomes difficult, if not impossible, to address storm water runoff in a meaningful way.

In Chicago, where Mayor Richard Daley has emerged as the leading proponent of green roofs, 1.6 million square feet (150,000 square meters) of green roof are in the pipeline (Peck 2005). Daley and other forward-looking

A raised bed on the building roof is prepared for planting.

elected leaders, such as Baltimore Mayor Martin O'Malley and US Senator Barbara A. Mikulski of Maryland, know that the infrastructures of cities and suburban areas aren't likely to change or reconfigure dramatically, so greening strategies such as green roofs hold special promise for simultaneously addressing multiple problems that arise in conjunction with development and that affect daily life for increasing numbers of people.

In areas with high concentrations of gaseous and particulate matter from cars and trucks, factories, and pollens and dust, plant leaves absorb impurities, contributing to improved air quality. Where vegetation is lacking, pollutants eventually are absorbed untreated into the ground water or, if they settle on buildings or other impervious surfaces, simply collect in layers of grime. When they land on a plant, by contrast, the plant's leaves absorb the gaseous pollutants and particulate matter is broken down by soil microbes, removing it from the atmosphere.

Green roofs can also significantly extend the life of a roof by protecting its roofing membrane. This, in turn, reduces roofing costs in the long run. Because a green roof covers the roofing membrane with a series of layers, it protects it from the extreme temperature fluctuations and ultraviolet rays that degrade traditional exposed roofing membranes. By insulating a green roof's membrane from the heaving and cracking associated with normal roofs, an extensive green roof does not have to be replaced as frequently as a regular roof. Planning

Maryland Senator Barbara Mikulski, along with a young student and Baltimore Mayor Martin O'Malley, examine a plug that will be planted on the green roof of the Mikulski Workforce Development Center in Baltimore.

Plant leaves, such as those of *Sedum spurium* 'Fuldaglut', absorb gaseous pollutants that contribute to poor air quality.

for a 30 to 40–year green roof life span is common in Germany (Breuning 2005). Thus, while a green roof can cost about double that of a traditional roof due to the engineering and installation costs, it will pay for itself over time in savings for a replacement roof and on lower cooling costs over the life of the green roof. The energy savings accrue from the increased insulating properties of a vegetated structure, evaporative cooling from the vegetation itself, and the thermal mass effects of the substrate. Collectively, these attributes also combine to reduce the urban heat island effect that builds up as a result of paved roads and other impervious surfaces that reflect heat.

Green roofs can also potentially offset a building's total cost by allowing a larger developable footprint, one that would otherwise be devoted to detention ponds or other remediation measures that are mandated to compensate for an increase in impervious surface. As developable land becomes scarcer, green roofs will be an increasingly viable economic choice for builders and developers across North America, not just in Europe.

Green Roof Challenges

Their many benefits notwithstanding, green roofs present a number of challenges that must be understood and addressed if they are to succeed in North America as more than high-end amenities or environmental anomalies. First, the paradigm must shift away from thinking of green roofs as "regular" gardens, only elevated. They are not like regular gardens: unlike natural landscapes, green roofs have no equivalent in nature. They are engineered, fabricated systems and thus present unknowns for most landscape designers, architects, and installers. Failing to acknowledge this and adapt to the special constraints posed by green roofs, including its plant requirements, will only ensure an unsuccessful project. Load-bearing considerations, for example, are not usually a concern of garden experts, nor is the challenge of hauling plant material onto a roof. Questions of access to the roof are among the unique challenges faced by green roof landscapers. When a green roof is to be installed 20 stories above the ground and has only limited accessibility, then all materials, including medium and plants, as well as the laborers, must be transported to the site. This adds costs not usually associated with landscaping, and it may involve securing dedicated use of an elevator or hiring a crane to deliver the materials to the site. All of these challenges can be satisfactorily addressed, but they take planning that differs from that of the typical ground-level garden.

Most extensive roof gardens are strikingly different from ground-level gardens, both visually and functionally.

The typical ground-level perennial garden bears little resemblance to an extensive roof, mostly because its substrate is much deeper and richer.

Green roofs on high rises, such as this new installation on the National Bohemian Building in Baltimore, can present logistical challenges to transporting materials to the site.

The act of growing plants under atypical conditions necessarily influences their selection and maintenance in ways that differ from considerations for ground-level gardens. Selecting the right plants is one of the foremost challenges of green roof plantings. For example, without irrigation and at least 8 in. (20 cm) of mostly organic medium, most green roofs in North America cannot sustain the wide variety of plant species that appear in traditional gardens. Since extensive roofs are traditionally non-irrigated and consist mostly of lightweight, inorganic medium, a plant specification list for a green roof is quite different from one for a ground-level garden. This point cannot be overstated; most herbaceous perennials, including natives, that otherwise might work well for the hardiness zone of a given roof still will not be suitable for a green roof microclimate. In addition, the average inorganic green roof medium will not support most large root systems or their nutritional requirements, further limiting plant choices to those with shallow root systems and an ability to store water.

Other challenges for green roof plantings are inherent with higher installation costs and the fact that they take longer to realize a return on investment. Although European green roofs have proven cost effective in the long run, particularly in reducing energy usage in the summer months, no such data exists yet for North America. In Europe, especially in Germany and Switzerland, widespread environmental, economic, and public policies support green roofs; this is not true for North America, however. Such implementations will take years to develop and may take on entirely different emphases here. Because relatively few installations exist across North America at this time, reliable information about plant specifications for a variety of green roof scenarios is hard to come by. Equally important, finding experienced professionals to design,

Sedum dasyphyllum is exceptionally shallow rooted and well suited to extensive green roof planting.

install, and maintain green roofs is still not easy, and this can lead to unnecessary and costly mistakes.

Gradually, however, all this is beginning to change, as is the availability of products designed or adapted for the green roof market, including vegetated mats, modules, premixed medium, and complete roofing systems, most of which originate in Germany. All of those tools make installation simpler and less daunting to the novice, and the more readily they are available, the more quickly green roofs will gain a foothold in the North American market.

As in any new field, finding adequate data to support the benefits of green roofs is also a challenge. North America is just beginning the process of quantifying the benefits of greening roofs, and it will be years before their true impact will be known. Nonetheless, the process has begun; projects range from a Canadian partnership in Toronto (Peck 2005), to green roof trials at major US and Canadian research institutions, to installations that are still in the planning or growing phases on hundreds of roofs across the continent. Data collected during the early part of the twenty-first century will contribute to knowledge of how North American climatic conditions, which are generally more extreme than those of Europe, impact plant growth and mortality. More than just anecdotal evidence will buttress claims about prolonged roof life, increased insulation properties, and reduced energy costs. A clearer picture of the economics of engineering and installing green

Green roof trials at major universities, including this one at Penn State University, provide much needed data on the environmental benefits of green roofs.

roofs compared to their value will predict whether they will become more attractive to short-term investors, whose only interest may be economic.

These challenges are not insignificant. If the market continues to grow, however, and if the successes of Europe are even partially transferable, the impact of green roofs will be far reaching and profoundly felt on the North American continent.

CHAPTER 2
Green Roof Design and Construction

A T ITS MOST ELEMENTAL, a green roof consists of introduced plants or
seeds that grow in some type of medium on a roof. Modern green
roofs, however, while not always complicated, are far from rudimen-
tary. Both extensive green roofs, which typically consist of 1 to 6 in. (2.5 to
15 cm) of lightweight, predominantly inorganic medium, and intensive
green roofs, which often employ more than 12 in. (30 cm) of soil and more
closely approximate traditional ground-level gardens, require engineered systems to ensure proper functioning. Thus, while each green roof is unique, all
share common components, including waterproofing, insulation, filtration,
and drainage layers; some type of root barrier; planting medium; and plant
material. If any one of those elements is missing or fails, whether due to a
roof leak or plant mortality caused by standing water, too little water, or inadequate medium, the green roof itself will ultimately fail.

Because the practical challenges associated with creating and repairing
green roofs can be daunting, rooftop failures are invariably more complex
and costly than failures on the ground. With that in mind, proper engineering, planning, design, and installation of green roofs are essential. Two
sources that cover these components in comprehensive detail are Nigel Dunnett and Nöel Kingsbury's *Planting Green Roofs and Living Walls* and Theo-
dore Osmundson's *Roof Gardens: History, Design, and Construction*. An additional excellent resource is Germany's Landscape Research, Development
and Construction Society (Forschungsgesellschaft Landschaftsentwicklung
Landschaftsbau, or FLL), which developed the comprehensive standards for
the installation of green roofs and has made them available in English (FLL
2002).

Determine and Plan for the Green Roof's Primary Purpose

Articulating a green roof's purpose and incorporating that into the early stages
of planning and design is critical. The client, building owner, architect, roof-

ing professional, local zoning officials, horticulturist, and landscape architect need to work as a team to discuss the needs and intents of the design. In so doing, they must factor in everything from budget and maintenance constraints to accessibility, safety, plant selection criteria, desired characteristics, and the logistics of installation. Because green roofs can potentially serve multiple ends, establishing and designing for a roof's primary use is essential. The following questions should be considered: Is it designed for storm water management, including water retention? Is temperature management, including mitigation of the urban heat island effect, a desired outcome? Is the roof primarily aesthetic, so that bloom times and colors are most important? Is it meant to be used as recreational space or to accommodate significant foot traffic?

All of the ends may be compatible, but each requires different design and structural emphases and will significantly impact how the roof looks and functions, including what vegetation will cover it. A commercial designer

The Eden Project in Cornwall, England, features green roofs that serve many purposes, but their primary mission is ecological education; school groups and other visitors are drawn from around the world. Photograph by Lucie L. Snodgrass.

seeking storm water credits from a local zoning jurisdiction, for example, should place more emphasis on using plants that store maximum amounts of water, such as hardy succulents, than on plants that may be visually pleasing, such as delphiniums, but that are inappropriate for extensive roofs. The two are not always at odds, but they can be, and green roofs should be designed with these considerations in mind. In other instances, a green roof might be installed as a draw or amenity for ecologically minded tenants. This was the case in the Montgomery Park building in Baltimore, Maryland, where the existence of a green roof and a wide array of other environmentally beneficial features on the warehouse rehabilitation project secured the Maryland Department of the Environment as its primary tenant. An additional benefit of that same project was an enormous amount of positive attention in the press, helping the developer to fill the building and create regional interest in green roofs.

A green roof planned exclusively for an inaccessible residential garage, for example, will require load-bearing specifications that differ significantly from those of roofs intended as accessible demonstration projects, such as the Chicago and Toronto city halls. Public use might also dictate a diversity of plantings and bloom periods that a largely functional roof doesn't require, which in turn might determine whether the green roof needs an irrigation system to allow for a greater variety of plant species. All of these issues influence and, indeed, drive the design process. Regardless of the goals, however, all of them must be incorporated early in the process, so that the design components are complementary and not at cross purposes.

The green roof on the Montgomery Park building in Baltimore has drawn environmentally conscious tenants to the renovated office park.

Budget constraints must also be incorporated early into the design phase of the project. The cost of a green roof is influenced by site-specific considerations such as slope, materials, kinds and sizes of plants, depth and composition of medium, amount of plants used, and building, installation, and maintenance costs. The life span of the plants and the roof itself will also play a role in determining budget. A 30 to 40–year roof is possible with proper waterproofing, installation, and maintenance.

Load-bearing Considerations

Load bearing is the most critical consideration for any green roof. While extensive roofs are generally lighter than intensive roofs and are engineered accordingly, the load-bearing or dead-load requirements are higher than those of a roof designed only to meet local building codes.

Structural engineers assess loads from two general perspectives: dead and live loads. Local building codes usually specify a roof's required live load, which includes snow, water, wind, and safety factors required for the building's performance. Live load also includes human traffic, temporary instal-

Planting a green roof on a steeply pitched surface, such as this one on an office building in Stuttgart, Germany, can increase installation costs if special accommodations are necessary to prevent slippage of the medium and plants.

lations such as furniture or maintenance equipment, and anything else of a transient nature. Dead load includes the weight of the roof itself, along with any permanent elements that make up the roof's structure, including the roofing layers, any permanent mechanical installations for heating or cooling, and the projected wind or snow loads. Green roofs must be designed to withstand both live and dead loads. Additionally, because extensive green roof systems must be evaluated while fully saturated—which adds from 15 to 25 pounds per square foot—this must also be factored in.

Load requirements will vary according to a number of additional considerations: whether the structure for the green roof is new or existing; whether it is intended for a flat or pitched surface; local climatic conditions such as snow, rain, and wind; and the depth and composition of the medium. Lightweight systems with substrate depths between 2 and 6 in. (5 to15 cm) typically increase the roof's dead load by 14 to 35 pounds per square foot, while intensive green roofs call for dead load requirements of between 59 and 199 pounds per square foot (Dunnett and Kingsbury 2004). In light of the design and structural load calculation requirements needed to determine dead and live loads, a structural engineer should be a member of the design team. In the case of an existing building, a structural engineer should always re-

Sloped roofs, such as this one on a chiropractic office in Hazelton, Pennsylvania, make fine candidates for green roofs with some modifications.

view the original drawings for the building and ascertain what load adjustments are necessary to accommodate the green roof.

On both new construction and retrofit projects, building construction and material selections predict the fundamental success or failure of the entire project. The earlier a green roof is incorporated into a design plan, the less costly it will be. Retrofitting an existing structure is considerably more expensive than designing a green roof as a part of new construction. Where retrofitting is necessarily a part of a project, ensuring that the existing roof is properly engineered for the additional weight will avoid the most serious of all green roof failures: collapse. Ideally, on new buildings, the green roof should be carefully considered in the site design phase to take advantage of any overall economies that the green roof might accrue, such as eliminating or reducing a detention pond or other storm water management facilities.

After load has been properly calculated and incorporated into a roof's design, a green roof is theoretically possible on a variety of slopes. Although the vast majority of green roofs are installed on almost flat roofs (with slope ratios of 0.25:12 to 2:12, which equals 1.2 to 9.5 degrees, or 2 to 17 percent, respectively), installing green roofs on pitched roofs is common, even on steeply sloped surfaces. Design considerations must be adjusted for sloped green roofs above 3:12 (14 degrees, or 25 percent), however, because they require special stabilization measures to reduce slippage (Dunnett and Kingsbury 2004). A variety of baffling, grids, strips, and other measures can be employed to hold the plants and medium in place.

Components of the Green Roof

The term *green roof* actually denotes a system comprising several components, or layers, that work together to function as a single, combined unit. For example, while a green roof can be built on a variety of decking surfaces, including concrete, steel, wood, and composite, the system is possible only when other components are added to ensure that the roof is protected against collapse and degradation and several other conditions are met. Assuming, for example, that load-bearing issues have been addressed, a green roof would still not be possible unless it included all—not just some—of the following components: decking, a waterproofing layer, an insulation layer, a root barrier, a drainage layer, a filter layer, and a substrate or medium layer.

In considering which system might work best, one must evaluate the system as a whole to ensure that it meets all of the required needs. Fortu-

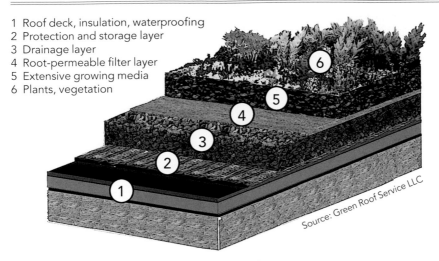

1 Roof deck, insulation, waterproofing
2 Protection and storage layer
3 Drainage layer
4 Root-permeable filter layer
5 Extensive growing media
6 Plants, vegetation

Source: Green Roof Service LLC

Functional layers of a typical extensive green roof. Drawing courtesy of Jörg Breuning.

nately, numerous and varied roofing systems are available on today's market, most of them originating in Germany, and all feature the necessary components. All of a system's components must be designed for a similar life span, so that no single layer fails prematurely and necessitates replacement of the entire system.

Deck layer

The first and most essential layer on a green roof is its decking, which can be constructed from concrete, wood, metal, plastic, gypsum, or composite. Plywood, the most common roof deck construction for residential projects in North America, has less structural strength than concrete or metal, the materials of choice on most commercial projects. Plywood is thus most likely to require additional engineering to support a green roof (Gaulin 2005). Buildings with concrete decks are excellent candidates for green roofs because they are stronger to begin with and because the decking does not degrade in the same way that wood does. Metal decks are normally corrugated and, while strong and well suited for green roofs, will require support for the waterproofing membrane since insulation is required. This support is usually installed over the corrugated decking and is capable of supporting the weight of the green roof.

Waterproofing layer

An effective and reliable waterproofing layer is the next critical factor, without which the green roof cannot succeed. The waterproofing membrane

Testing for roof leaks on a soon-to-be-planted green roof should be included in every project plan.

must be 100 percent waterproof. Any weakness or failure in the membrane can be difficult to detect because it will be entirely covered; repairing leaks may require removal of the entire system, including plants and medium, and should be avoided at all costs. The extra time and effort spent ensuring an effective and durable seal are well worth the cost.

Considerable debate surrounds the best methods and systems of waterproofing, which fall into many categories: the built-up roof, modified bitumen, single-ply, and the liquid applied methods (Osmundson 1999). Built-up roofs comprise multiple layers of organic or synthetic felts layered with hot asphalt. The life span of built-up roofs, however, is limited to 20 to 30 years, which is undesirable for green roofs, and they are vulnerable to cracks and blistering caused by moisture and temperature extremes. Modified bitumen roofs consist of reinforced synthetic modified asphalt sheets that are torched, adhered, or set in hot asphalt; self-adhered modified bitumen membranes are also available. Single-ply membranes consist of rolled sheets of inorganic materials made from plastic, PVC, TPO membrane, or synthetic rubber, usually with heat-welded seams. They perform very well in green roof applications if properly installed and if all seams are correctly checked for secure welding. Single-ply membranes are also naturally root resistant and do not require additional root barriers. Liquid-applied membranes, whether sprayed or painted, hot or cold, can provide a seamless application, but they are most often applied on a solid concrete deck. The many liquid-applied materials, methods, thicknesses, and qualities should be researched prior to selection. One of the advantages of materials directly adhered to concrete, whether rubberized asphalt, modified membrane, or liquid urethane, is that if a leak or damage occurs, water migration or traveling will not occur and the leak can easily be traced. Whatever method of waterproofing is used,

A single-ply membrane roof is used on a new building at Swarthmore College in Swarthmore, Pennsylvania.

many available, additional layers can be added for insulation or other protection. PVC or other polypropylene products work well for those purposes (Gaulin 2005).

Insulation layer

Proper insulation for the roof will govern many of the energy savings advantages green roofs offer. Insulation is achieved either under the membrane or on top of the membrane, which is known as an inverted roof membrane assembly (IRMA) system. IRMA roofs consist of a deck, then a waterproofing membrane, then insulation, and finally the other green roof layers. As a whole, the trend in building is to move the insulation to the outside of the building, in part to avoid mildew problems that are common in wet areas. The advantage of an IRMA system is that the membrane is fully protected, greatly hindering mechanical penetration of the roof. In addition, the IRMA system avoids thermal shock caused by wide variances in temperature at the membrane level, and it protects the membrane from UV degradation.

Protection and storage layer

Because green roofs incorporate living and growing materials, a protection and storage layer—a root barrier—is also among the elements needed, and it is one element that should never be compromised. If a roof deck is made of an organic material—whether wood, asphalt, bitumen, or any other biodegradable product—the root barrier must be placed above the waterproofing membrane to ensure that no vegetation can breach it and undermine the entire system. Root-repellent systems are most often made from PVC or HDPE (high-density polyethylene) sheets, although they can also employ sheets with copper or other chemical impregnation. A variety of roofing systems are available, most originating in Germany; but they are increasingly available in North America as more suppliers enter the market every year.

Drainage layer

The green roof must also have a well-functioning drainage system that allows excess water from the plants' roots to be removed as quickly as possible. Proper drainage is critical both for the roof and the health of the plants. Flat roofs are especially susceptible to standing water, and plant material will quickly rot without a well-draining medium or engineered drainage system built into the roof's membrane. Ensuring that water drains away from the roots of the plants can be accomplished through the medium itself on most extensive roofs, especially on sloping roofs and where rainfall is limited. For areas that receive excessive moisture, however, or where conditions are not conducive to adequate drainage, man-made drainage systems are readily available, often as part of a complete roofing system. A variety of available systems can be quite elaborate and include water storage cups or lightweight

A drainage system overgrown with plant material can lead to standing water and root rot, causing plant mortality.

Boxing in the drain and keeping it vegetation free will ensure that it functions well for years to come.

plastic modules, while others are much more straightforward. The type and extent of the drainage system will be determined by site-specific considerations, such as load-bearing capacity, building height, and budget.

Man-made medium is typically lighter than a natural medium, an advantage if the material is being transported to a roof 20 stories high. In situations like those in coastal zones with heavy winds, a heavier drainage system medium utilizing stone chips, scoria, or expanded clay will better withstand wind uplift, which can cause damage to ballasted roofs.

Root-permeable filter layer

Whether the system relies on the medium to drain the water or a man-made system, some type of filter cloth or mat must also be included—most likely a semi-permeable polypropylene fabric. This mat separates the medium from the drainage layer, avoiding clogging (Dunnett and Kingsbury 2004) and protecting the medium from moving off the roof and washing down the drain. Filter cloths can be a part of the drainage system and adhered to it, or they can provide a completely separate layer.

Growing medium layer

Finally, the roof will need a medium or substrate in which to grow plants. Unlike ground-level gardens that rely on rich organic materials, extensive green roof plants need to grow in a lightweight medium that is porous, that

Tiny, newly planted cuttings grow on a Stuttgart roof in a largely inorganic medium made from recycled construction and industrial waste, including clay roofing tiles and steel mill slag.

holds oxygen and water and absorbs and retains nutrients, and that provides some stability for the plants' root systems. These are difficult and sometimes opposing goals to achieve, and yet they must be in balance; for example, using a medium that leads to standing water ensures plenty of moisture but no air, which leads to root rot. In addition, prolonged exposure to standing water can in some cases compromise the integrity of the entire roofing system. The substrate for most extensive green roofs should be largely inorganic, in part because it helps maintain vertical integrity and avoid shrinkage, but also because a highly organic medium adds weight and nutrients, each of which can be problematic.

The ideal extensive roof substrate should consist of 75 to 90 percent inorganic, weed-free medium (Beattie and Berghage 2004). Materials particularly suited to extensive roofs include expanded slate, expanded shale, expanded clay, baked clay, volcanic pumice, scoria, sand, and crushed clay roofing tiles, which are used most often in Germany. The remainder of the medium should be organic compost—not soil, which contains silt and can block the filter cloth and disrupt the drainage system. Cumulatively, the medium should experience very little compaction and should anchor the

A mixture of expanded shale and compost is poured onto a roof in preparation for planting.

plants, retain moisture and some nutrients, and be porous. The exact mix will be determined by the types of plants intended for the roof, the climatic conditions on the site, weight loads, and drainage needs. The medium should also be pH neutral or close, and it should be applied when damp to avoid wind loss.

The depth of the medium must also be considered, as it impacts a number of factors, including plant selection and growth rate. Substrate on extensive roofs is rarely deeper than 6 in. (15 cm), largely due to load-bearing constraints, and is made up largely of inorganic materials, which limits plant selection from the outset. Within those parameters, however, is a significant variation in plant viability between 2 and 6 in. (5 and

Clockwise from upper left, pumice, expanded slate, expanded clay, and expanded shale all work well as green roof media.

To grow grasses on a roof with only 4 in. (10 cm) of medium throughout, the material is mounded in one area, adding several inches to the depth.

15 cm) of medium and in substrate with relatively more or less organic material. While a single species of *Sedum* may do very well in 2 in. (5 cm) of inorganic substrate, for example, plants with deeper root systems and higher nutrient requirements, such as grasses, will not fare as well. Achieving the correct mix and depth is a delicate balance, and in North America, which lags behind Europe in mature installations, gaining a true understanding of the best media and depths for a variety of conditions will take some time.

As with the other layers of the green roof, the planting medium should be designed for a long-term life span of 40 to 50 years, partly to maximize the return on investment but also to avoid having to tear up the entire green roof to replant it. As with all of the other components of the green roof structure, knowledge and workmanship cannot be separated from the materials used.

CHAPTER 3

Vegetation and Plant Selection

G REEN ROOF PLANTING DESIGNERS must consider multiple criteria when planning a design, including design intent; the client's needs and expected outcomes; budget and maintenance parameters; life expectancy of the green roof; access and safety issues; location; micro and macro-environments; exposure; humidity or dryness; maximum and minimum temperatures; medium weight, depth, and composition; and irrigation. Careful plant selection is essential to the green roof's success, as traditional rules used for ground-level plant selection simply won't work on a roof. By necessity, green roof plants must be tougher and less nutrient-reliant than plants found in most gardens.

The type of planting medium used is also particularly significant. Organic content, pH and nutrient levels, weight, porosity, and water retention capacity all need to be evaluated, just as they would in a regular garden. But because of its location, the green roof medium must be substantially lighter, less rich, and more porous than soil used for a ground-level garden. The Landscape Research, Development and Construction Society (FLL) guidelines for green roofs discuss medium composition at length, and the FLL publication *Guideline for the Planning, Execution and Upkeep of Green-Roof Sites* (2002) is an excellent planning resource. FLL medium certification is also available through Penn State University (Beattie 2005).

Environment and geography also influence plant selection. Design professionals responsible for plant specification must be knowledgeable about the heat and hardiness zones in which the green roof is planted and what plants normally thrive in those zones. In addition, site-specific considerations for a green roof are far more localized than those that appear on any map. Most high and low temperature hardiness zone maps are based on 25-year average low and high temperatures (White 2005), and they do not account for microclimates that are created due to shade, the urban heat island effect, structures that affect the microclimates, increases or decreases in humidity, and other factors. Plant selection for green roofs must be based on all of these climatic conditions, including exposure to sunlight, wind, shade, and temperature fluctuations.

The effect of elevating gardens to the roof level can lead to particular stresses on plant material, due to the decreased substrate thickness. In addition, sun, heat, and wind are more damaging to plants on a roof and can lead to plant stress and eventual mortality. While the effects of heat stress are not as immediate as those of freezing temperatures, stunted growth and plant mortality can and do result from overexposure to heat. Regional differences in the intensity of eight hours of exposure to sunlight per day will also influence plant specification. A sunny day in Boston, for example, will generally provide different levels of irradiance and humidity than a sunny day in Phoenix, and plants must be selected accordingly.

In general terms, the most successful green roof plants are low-growing, shallow-rooted perennial plants that are heat, cold, sun, wind, drought, salt, insect, and disease tolerant. At the same time, in most of the green roof market in North America, plants must also be able to tolerate some wet roots, especially on lower sections of steeply sloped roofs and on flat roofs during the winter. Green roof plants should also have a long life expectancy or the ability to self propagate, and they should require minimal nutrients and maintenance (White 2005). Plants that are highly flammable, that develop large root systems and thus a high biomass, or that are excessively "thirsty"

Assorted sedum and other hardy succulents grow in a mostly inorganic medium.

should be avoided. Plants that require a high amount of nutrients should also be avoided, because they can exacerbate nutrient loading in the riparian systems, adding to, rather than reducing, runoff-related pollution (Hunt 2005).

Since most green roof medium is fractured, or lacking a continuous column of water that facilitates capillary action, it is difficult for water reservoirs residing at the bottom of the medium to move up into the plant root zone. As a result, green roof plants must be able to withstand periods of dryness and heat, a factor that eliminates most traditional annuals and perennials. In the southwestern and western United States, as well as in Latin America, heat and drought are recurring and enduring problems; this adds even more to the challenge of specifying plants that will flourish in those areas. In drought-prone areas, specifying drought-tolerant plants may not be enough; irrigation systems may need to be installed to ensure plant survival—not only during establishment, but for the long term. Design professionals planning a green roof must consider local needs and realize that roofs at higher elevations will experience more intense heat and wind and lower medium moisture levels.

On the other hand, excessive moisture can quickly lead to stress and mortality, particularly for common green roof plants such as *Sedum* and

Sedum ternatum thrives in the shade and is especially well suited to roofs that receive a lot of moisture.

This poorly placed drainage pipe results in excessive moisture on the green roof, encouraging root rot and the introduction of weeds.

Delosperma. It can also create a beneficial germination climate for weed seeds. Hence, only certain plant species are suitable for green roofs and then only in conjunction with a carefully planned system that ensures adequate drainage, the optimal medium, and, where necessary or desired, an irrigation system to keep the plants alive.

Plant Types for Green Roofs

Plants are usually classified as annuals, biennials, or perennials, based on their yearly and continuing growth cycles. Annuals grow, flower, set seed, and die in one growing season. Biennials grow vegetation the first growing season, and then they flower, set seed, and die the second growing season. Biennials are not generally used on green roofs, as they create gaps in the roofscape after they finish blooming and die. Perennials grow, flower, and set seed in one or more growing seasons, and they do not die after setting seed.

The combined constraints governing plant selection for green roofs eliminate the vast majority of annual and perennial plants associated with traditional gardens, including many native plants. Although some herbaceous perennials and annuals may be used as accent plants or for seasonal interest in carefully selected locations with an appropriately deep medium and proper irrigation, they should not make up the bulk of plants specified for an extensive green roof.

Annuals

Annuals should not be the dominant plant selection for the majority of extensive green roofs because they do not offer the requisite longevity required

Phacelia campanularia blooms a vivid blue and naturally reseeds, making this annual a popular accent plant on green roofs.

to make a project cost effective. They can be incorporated into plant specifications as seasonal accents, provided the medium and the green roof system will support them. Where annuals are used extensively, regular rainfall of at least 3 in. (7.5 cm) per month is required, and even then the plants may require a supplemental irrigation system. Drought-tolerant annuals such as *Portulaca* in the southern US or *Phacelia cam-*

panularia or *Townsendia eximia* may be used on extensive green roofs as fillers to provide quick color during the first growing season, or they can be used if they naturally reseed without becoming invasive.

Herbaceous perennials

For aesthetic reasons, herbaceous perennials are the most desired plants for extensive green roofs. They offer the greatest color, texture, and seasonal variability, but they require deeper substrate and moisture than are found on most extensive green roofs. Most herbaceous perennials also have limited drought tolerance or ability to withstand the stresses of the green roof, and the deep roots of many taxa make most herbaceous perennials poor choices for green roofs. Some, however, can work well on extensive green roof installations. *Petrorhagia* can be used, for example, as can some species of *Dianthus*, *Phlox*, *Campanula*, *Teucreum*, *Allium*, *Potentilla*, *Achillea*, *Prunella*, *Viola*, *Origanum*, and other low-growing, shallow-rooted perennials. When using taller herbaceous perennials as the primary plant material, however, the medium depth must be increased to greater than 4 in. (10 cm) and adequate or supplementary water sources for the plants must be available. Regional considerations are also important when using perennials—for ex-

Dianthus, seen here growing with *Sedum sexangulare*, is among the most successful herbaceous perennials for use on green roofs.

Oxalis is an enthusiastic interloper on green roofs that employ a deeper, more organic medium than those on typical extensive roofs.

ample, 6 in. (15 cm) of medium in Portland, Oregon, will support more varied vegetation than 6 in. (15 cm) of medium in Houston, Texas, due to the differences in rainfall averages and distribution.

Herbaceous perennials must be chosen carefully for compatibility relative to site-specific considerations. While perennials make it possible to achieve a wider palette of plant material with the requisite accommodations, as they expand in biomass they also increase roof load by 2 to 5 pounds per square foot. In addition, the richer medium required by most herbaceous perennials creates a more hospitable climate for weeds, which may crowd out the specified plants and add to after-installation costs for maintenance. In a city housing authority complex in Portland, Oregon, for example, clover took over most of the green roof because of the relatively high organic content in the 5 in. (12.5 cm) medium and because no action was taken to eradicate the clover once it became established (Beattie 2005). If a deep medium is specified, selected herbicides may be required as part of a maintenance routine to keep weeds in check.

Relatively few herbaceous perennials are evergreen, so if winter interest is a major design consideration for a roof, an alternative must be provided to compensate for the long stretches of brown vegetation visible during the plants' dormant period. In addition, many herbaceous perennials, such as *Penstemon*, have limited longevity to begin with, and this can be further truncated depending on medium depth, environmental factors, disease or insect susceptibility, and ecological competition. A careful designer must specify perennials that are long lived in addition to drought and heat tolerant. Currently, no data exists to suggest that herbaceous perennials in North America can survive in less than 4 in. (10 cm) of medium—even those choices are limited to low-growing plants such as *Petrorhagia*, *Campanula rotundifolia*, and various *Phlox* and *Carex* species.

Salvia, Prunella, and *Campanula* species combine with hardy succulents to form a dense carpet.

Hardy succulents

Hardy succulents are the workhorses of extensive roofs and the primary plants for systems using a medium of 4 in. (10 cm) or less in most areas. These plants have an unsurpassed ability to survive drought and wind conditions, store water in their leaves for extended periods, and conserve water through a unique metabolic process known as *Crassulacean acid metabolism* (CAM). These plants can reduce water loss by opening their stomates during the night, storing carbon dioxide for photosynthesis, and then closing their stomates during the day, thus reducing losses from transpiration. Many such plants are classified as *facultative* CAM, meaning they will undergo the CAM process only if water is limited (Stephenson 1994). These xerophytes, or xeric plants, are characterized by shallow root systems and can survive extended periods of drought as well as other temperature extremes, including cold (White 2005).

Hardy succulents, in general, and *Sedum, Sempervivum, Talinum, Jovibarba,* and *Delosperma,* specifically, are the obvious and, in some cases, the only choices for thin substrate, non-irrigated, extensive roof gardens, with *Sedum* showing the greatest survivability in a wide range of conditions.

Clients and designers alike often require a wider plant palette than simply hardy succulents. In part, this stems from an assumption that the choices among hardy succulents are severely limited, but that is not accurate. With nearly 600 species of *Sedum* alone, the choices among hardy succulents are diverse and extensive and offer year-round visual interest. Depending on location, a well-planned North American green roof can feature *Sedum* in flower from March to November (Stephenson 1994).

Commonly known as stonecrop, orpine, or livelong, sedums exist as annuals, biennials, triennials, perennials, or herbaceous species, but most are inhabitants of the Northern Hemisphere, found in well-drained areas with little vegetative competition (Stephenson 1994). In North America, sedums thrive in hardiness zones 3 to 9a. As a genus, *Sedum* is usually a low-growing, spreading groundcover with pink, white, or yellow flowers, although some species can reach up to 3 ft. (1 m) in height. Sedums are sometimes characterized by tight, red to evergreen rosettes that change color with the seasons and provide a degree of winter interest—a characteristic most other perennials do not share. They are generally long lived and are self-propagating or rerooting plants, although some perennial sedums will act as annuals under

Sempervivum species can withstand long periods of heat and drought and require very shallow medium for survival.

The broad range of hardy succulents suitable for extensive green roofs includes *Orostachys boehmeri*.

extreme stress, using all of their energy to produce viable seed for survival. All of these characteristics—especially their ability to withstand temperature extremes—make them ideal for green roofs.

In a three-year green roof trial (2001 to 2004) conducted by researchers at Michigan State University utilizing 4 in. (10 cm) of growing substrate composed of 60 percent heat-expanded slate, nine *Sedum* species vastly out-performed eighteen Michigan natives in every instance (Monterusso et al. 2005). While some other taxa survived, including *Allium cernuum*, *Coreopsis lanceolata*, and *Tradescantia ohiensis*, most of the Michigan natives without supplemental irrigation did not, while all nine species of *Sedum* survived and provided 100 percent coverage. The Michigan natives did well when irrigated, but irrigation adds maintenance and cost

The bright red leaves of *Sedum* ×*rubro-tinctum* provide jewel-like counterpoints to other plants.

Rugged sedums, including *Sedum album*, *S. kamtschaticum* var. *floriferum* 'Weihen-stephaner Gold', and *S. spurium* 'Fuldaglut', create dramatic colors swaths on a sloped green roof.

considerations and is normally not provided on extensive green roofs. In another experiment (Van Woert et al. 2005a), *Sedum* survived 88 days without water, although the plants did not grow during that time of drought stress.

Their ability to survive in challenging conditions make sedums highly appropriate for green roof use. They also bloom profusely with a wide variety of bloom and leaf color and textures, are non-invasive, and are well loved by insects and birds. Sedums exist in many colors, from light green to red to purple, and they grow to various heights, from ground-hugging species to those suitable for border plantings in traditional gardens.

Talinum, a native plant in the Portulacaceae family commonly known as fameflower, encompasses nearly 50 species found mostly in North America (according to *Hortus Third*). *Talinum* is very drought hardy and handsome, and it blooms for months on end, although it is still considered ephemeral, so it leaves gaps in the landscape once it dies back. Still, it is extremely viable from seed and will readily establish itself in new places. *Talinum* is best used in conjunction with taxa that provide year-round interest. Most *Talinum* is self sowing, making it useful as an annual in areas typically colder than its designated hardiness zone.

Delosperma is widely used on green roofs in temperate zones, and, like *Talinum*, it is most often an everblooming perennial. More ornamental than

Talinum calycinum, shown here at the peak of its summer bloom, self seeds each year, providing visual interest for months at a time.

Sedum, the South African sun-lover blooms for months in brilliant shades of yellow, pink, coral, or white. *Delosperma* is limited in range, however, by its drought and cold tolerance—less than that of *Sedum*. Most *Delosperma* is not hardy past zone 7 in areas with wet winters, and the genus is highly susceptible to rot when exposed to standing water or excessive moisture. The genus has proven reliably hardy in Denver, Colorado (zone 5), which has mostly dry winters, while plants died in winter trials in East Lansing, Michigan, and State College, Pennsylvania. In green roof trials conducted by North Carolina State outside of Raleigh, *Delosperma* did exceptionally well in a 55 percent expanded slate substrate in 2002, a drought year, but it held

up less well in more typical years 2003 and 2004, whereas *Sedum mexicanum* thrived equally in all three years (Hunt 2005).

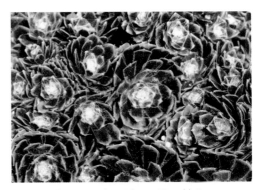

Sempervivum and *Jovibarba*, both commonly called houseleek, hen and chick, or live forever, are also well suited to extensive green roofs and comprise more than 40 species and hundreds of cultivars. Characterized by dense basal rosettes, *Semper-*

Sempervivum arachnoideum 'Sparkle'

Yellow *Delosperma nubigenum* 'Basutoland' and pink *Delosperma* 'John Proffitt' are equally bold, long-term bloomers.

vivum and *Jovibarba* are best specified as accents as they are relatively slow growing and spread by offsets, so they are not suitable for use as ground-covers. They are also extremely drought tolerant and nutrient tolerant and are well suited to planting under eaves and peaks of roofs where conditions are harsh.

Grasses

While grasses have become tremendously popular for traditional landscaping, they are still new to green roofs, although they have their place. While not colorful bloomers like annuals or perennials or evergreen like sedums, grasses have a lot to offer. They add motion and texture, are more vertical than succulents, offer bird and insect habitat, and can provide limited winter interest when left unpruned. That said, grasses, like herbaceous perennials, require a deeper medium to accommodate their root systems and attain a larger biomass than succulents, which can affect load and pose a fire hazard during winter dormancy. Also, some grasses may undergo a dormant period

Bouteloua curtipendula

Grasses, including 16,000 *Festuca*, were planted in the 14 in. (35 cm) deep intensive green roof of the Vancouver Public Library's central branch. Photograph by Charles Cronen-weth, American Hydrotech.

Sesleria autumnalis

during the summer, creating brown spots in the roofscape, while others are dormant in the winter and if cut back will also leave bare areas. For the most part, the shorter grasses that are appropriate for extensive systems, such as *Festuca*, *Carex*, and *Deschampsia*, lack the height and winter structure that tall grasses provide for gardens at ground level.

Like many perennials, grasses require some maintenance, including hard pruning before the onset of new growth, which necessitates that the roof be accessible for maintenance. Keeping the constraints in mind, some good options for grasses on green roofs with appropriate depths of medium include *Andropogon*, *Bouteloua*, *Carex*, *Sesleria*, and *Sporobolus*.

Herbs

Thymus, *Origanum*, *Salvia*, and *Allium* all have their selected uses on green roofs, as do some other herbs, although thymes and oreganos typically require more than 4 in. (10 cm) of medium and an irrigation system to provide the requisite moisture to help them root. Once established, many herbs are

The roof of the Fairmont Hotel in Vancouver is planted with a kitchen herb garden used by the hotel's restaurants.

drought tolerant, depending on geographic region. *Allium cernuum* survived and multiplied in a study of natives versus *Sedum* at Michigan State University (Monterusso et al. 2005), although the *A. cernuum* on the roof were only about half the size of the same plants growing in a much deeper medium in the surrounding landscape. Alliums and other herbs can work well on roofs of private residences or on restaurants, hospitals, or other institutional buildings, where they can be grown and harvested for culinary, aromatic, therapeutic, or educational purposes.

Bulbs, corms, and rhizomes

A limited number of geophytes are suitable for use on green roofs in areas with wet and cool spring seasons. The thin medium does not support larger bulbs, however, so the successful types tend to be dwarf irises, alliums, tulips, daffodils, grape hyacinths (*Muscari* spp.), and crocuses.

Seasonal flowering or evergreen plants

Plant specifications must take into consideration whether the roof requires year-round visual interest. Herbaceous perennials have a limited flowering period and lose their leaves during winter, while hardy succulents usually feature evergreen and/or colored and textured foliage, which extends their aesthetic interest period to most of the year. This is especially true of *Sedum*, *Jovibarba*, and *Sempervivum*, many of which bloom at staggered times in

Allium will readily self sow and redistribute across a roof.

different colors, with seasonal foliage color changes. Seeded or plug annuals may self sow after their first year, but they will likely spread across the roof in a haphazard fashion. A mix of hardy succulents, herbaceous perennials, and annuals may be combined to achieve year-round interest.

Groundcovers Versus Accent Plants

Green roofs should consist of groundcovers predominantly, with a limited amount of accent plants. Groundcovers provide a rapid, reliable, and cost-effective spread over the roof, with plugs covering from 6 to 10 in. (15 to 25 cm) horizontally in the first year. Examples of groundcovers that work well on a variety of green roofs include *Sedum album*, *S. spurium* 'John Creech', *S. sexangulare*, *Petrorhagia saxifrage*, and *Phlox subulata*.

Accent plants such as *Dianthus* species, while visually spectacular during bloom, may not live more than five years on the roof. In addition, they do not spread as rapidly as groundcovers, more plants are required to cover an area, and they offer only seasonal interest. Still, examples of successful green roof accent plants include various cultivars of *Dianthus* and *Allium*, *Talinum calycinum*, *Sedum* 'Matrona', and *S. cauticola* 'Lidakense'. As part of a maintenance plan for accent plants, they may need to be replenished by periodic resowing.

As its name suggests, *Sedum album* 'Coral Carpet' is an excellent groundcover for use on most green roofs.

Planted together, *Sedum rupestre* 'Angelina' and *Dianthus* offer a striking mix of groundcover and accent plants.

Growth Forms and Patterns

Form and pattern affect design. Plants vary widely in growth and habit, from mounding, cushionlike, tufted, and carpetlike, to compact, low-growing, and spreading. They can be upright or procumbent. Most of the plants specified for green roofs should be low-density groundcovers that are fast growing and long lived and that spread between 6 and 10 in. (15 and 25 cm) in

Because of its unchecked spread, *Sedum sarmentosum* should not be specified for a green roof project unless the roof receives ongoing maintenance to keep it in check.

Hardscaping on this green roof, including edging and pavers, creates a striking layout that also checks unwanted growth.

the first year from plugs. That relatively rapid spread will allow slower growing, more upright plants such as *Allium* or grasses to be interspersed in the planting, as long as the plants are compatible. Generally, a combination of low and high-density species allows a desirable ecological mixture to develop, in which runners fill in the spaces between cushions. When using plants with varying horizontal growth rates, such as *Sedum spurium* and *Sempervivum* species, plants should be placed so that the slower growing plants are not overrun. One should never specify plants with an unchecked growth rate, such as *Sedum sarmentosum*, which will spread as much as 30 in. (75 cm) per year, unless that is the only species desired on the roof—or unless a regular maintenance plan is in place to contain it. Aggressive plants should be placed within colonies to avoid crowding out others.

Growth patterns can be maximized and controlled in several ways. One approach is to confine plants to desired areas with modules, edging, or pavers to keep their roots from mixing with adjacent species. This creates striking designs and patterns and can be emphasized even more by utilizing widely contrasting leaf colors or blooms. In a design encompassing specific patterns, a maintenance plan is crucial for keeping the integrity of the patterns intact. This may require cutting back certain plants, replanting others periodically, and making other adjustments. Shoots can also be pruned occasionally to keep them from creeping over the containment systems—this must be done carefully, however, as crowding plants may result in shortening their life span.

Shallow and Fibrous-Rooted Plants

Plant root depth can, to some extent, predict the success of a green roof. For example, plants found in desert climates frequently have deep taproots, but extensive green roofs are not hospitable for such plants, as the medium lacks the depth and stability to support deep-rooted plant species. Plants found in alpine rocks and scree, on the other hand, often have shallow, spreading roots and leaf cell tissues that resist desiccation (White 2005b). Not surprisingly, many

Shallow-rooted *Sempervivum* thrives in a natural alpine setting.

alpines thrive on green roofs. Still, the unique location and construction of a green roof differentiates the locale from any other environment. Alpine plants in their natural habitat, for example, generally experience cool day-time and nighttime temperatures and low humidity, whereas green roofs are most often found in urban areas that suffer from hot nights exacerbated by the urban heat island effect. When night temperatures remain high, plant respiration is increased, net photosynthesis is decreased, and the plants even-tually exhaust their sugar reserves and die prematurely (Berghage 2005). Hence, in selecting shallow-rooted plants, one must specify plants that are heat and drought tolerant as well.

Native Plants on Green Roofs

With local and regional ecosystems under attack from invasive exotic species and declining animal and insect species, native plants and green roofs seem like a good fit. Native plants have evolved and adapted to ecological and climatic niches throughout North America. They are highly resistant to damage from climate, indigenous disease, insects, and animals, and they

Native plants that grow in tough natural settings, like these Colorado mountain plants, may be candidates for green roofs, but only after trials determine their survivability.

provide a stable biodiversity that has been vital to human survival. But building successful native gardens depends on building plant communities that work together, and the conditions of extensive green roofs do not readily lend themselves to those communities, although they may accommodate species from a community. Thus, replicating a native prairie or a wildflower meadow may not be possible on a green roof, simply because it is not a native environment and cannot accommodate the spectrum of taxa that make up a prairie. If a native plant community is desired, the project should not be limited to the roof but should encompass the site as a whole. Native prairies also perpetuate themselves over time by fire, which is impractical on the top of buildings (Rowe 2005).

Bouteloua curtipendula and *Sporobolus heterolepis*, both native to the United States, are suitable for use on extensive roofs with at least 6 in. (15 cm) of medium.

Natives can also be susceptible to exotic pests and diseases, and they are not generally well suited to the extensive green roof environment. Problems arise when natives have difficulty adapting to the unique green roof construction, environment, and medium depth and type. Many native plants have evolved in deep soils of a particular structure and microbial and nutrient balance. It may be impossible to re-create these conditions on a roof given the restrictions of wind and sun exposure and limited medium depth and type. Shallow substrates, in particular, may not be suitable for many native prairie plants.

Sedum pulchellum is native to the southeastern United States, where in zones 5 and below, it will act as an annual.

Site-specific concerns

Salt spray or salt in mists in coastal areas and acid rain from industrial areas can affect plant species choices. Substrate salt concentrations can be monitored with soluble salt analyses. Acid rain can be beneficial or detrimental, depending on the pH requirements for a particular plant species. Some species grow best in acid substrate (pH 5.2 to 6.2), some grow best in limey or alkaline substrate (pH 7.0 to 7.8), but the majority grow best near neutral (pH 6.2 to 7.0). Yearly chemical analyses will assist in determining how best to maintain the desired nutrient/pH balance (White 2005a).

Awareness of areas where heat might accumulate is also important. In cold climates, heat accumulation may be beneficial, but in hot climates or during summers in cold climates, too much heat accumulation will be harmful for most plants. Stone or concrete buildings and parapet walls can store heat during sunny days and release this heat at night.

Wind—especially winter wind—can pose a major problem affecting drying of substrate and plant desiccation. If a plant's root system is out of balance with its plant shoot growth, plants may wilt or die from wind and high temperature effects, even with sufficient moisture in the substrate. In general, low-growing, carpet-type, succulent groundcovers are most resistant to the combined effects of wind, sun, heat, and cold.

Plant Specification

Successful plant specifications marry the expertise of growers, designers, and horticulturists with the site specifications, producing a list of plants that complete an elegant and practical design. A good plant specification list should also include plants that are readily available in the trade. The combined processes of bidding, purchasing, installing, establishing, and ongoing maintenance are all contingent on the appropriate plant specification, so special attention should be afforded to this phase of the project.

The specification process should begin with functional and site-specific questions, all of which must be answered before planting begins. Where is

Plant selections should be both attractive and practical.

the project? What are the light conditions at the site? Will irrigation be necessary? How high is the roof? Is the roof old or new? How much weight is it engineered to carry? Is it near an ocean and will it be affected by salt spray? Is the roof in an exposed or sheltered location? Do any other roofs drain on to it? From there, more detailed questions should be considered: Has the client set goals for the installation, such as storm water management? Does the client desire a particular color scheme or planting pattern? Substrate composition and depth must be ascertained, and a budget must be established for any maintenance needs.

Load-bearing considerations

Weight plays a critical role in plant specification. Steel, wood, concrete, or composite decks can be engineered to support any required load. Existing roofs in older cities were frequently designed to support a built-up waterproofing system that also included cinder or stone ballast. The weight of these systems is typically about 12 to 15 pounds per square foot. In these circumstances, simple extensive green roofs can be offered as replacement roofs without concern for structural enhancements. Also, in temperate and cooler climates, roofs must be designed to accommodate snow loads. As a result, these roofs are often structurally stiffer than roofs designed for warm climates. For this reason, it is generally easier to retrofit roofs in colder latitudes than in warmer ones (Miller 2005).

On a new construction project, the green roof should be designed from the building's inception. This avoids the extra work and added cost of retrofitting decks to bear the total load that extensive green roofs typically impose, which is somewhere between 15 to 24 pounds per square foot, saturated (Breuning 2005a). This will vary somewhat with the plants and medium used.

Medium composition and depth

Composition of the underlying medium will also influence load and plant specification, depending on weight, water absorption capacity, and drainage rates. The ideal medium is relatively lightweight and retains water well, but it is also porous and freely draining; the more water the medium retains, the more weight it adds to the roof. The medium must also supply and absorb nutrients, anchor the plants, provide enough weight to avoid floating when wet or avoid being blown off during and after establishment, and retain most of its volume (Dunnett and Kingsbury 2004).

The medium used on the green roof of the Daimler-Chrysler engine factory in Stuttgart is a mix of crushed clay roofing tiles and recycled steel mill slag.

Generally, the ideal extensive roof medium is a blend of sandy or granular materials that balances water absorption with adequate porous surface. A variety of natural and man-made materials can be mixed to achieve the requisite balance, including lava, volcanic scoria, Lelite, pumice, diatomaceous earth, sand, expanded and active clays, expanded shale, gravel, bricks, and tiles. Vermiculite and perlite can be used in conjunction with other materials, but lightweight aggregates are both more expensive and less environmentally friendly than purely natural medium and must be evaluated in an economic context as well (Breuning 2005b). In addition, all green roof media must be able to withstand the freeze/thaw cycles of colder climates. Crushed concrete should be avoided entirely as it can clog a roof's drainage layers.

It is certainly true that the deeper and more organic the medium, the more planting options are available. Still, a predominantly organic medium is not recommended for extensive green roofs; while it increases fertility, it also introduces a set of potential problems, including decreased pore space, higher water retention, increased nutrient loading, and reduced medium depth over time, caused by decomposition. Any significant decrease in medium depth will change the design of the green roof and possibly create a need for additional substrate. Medium depth should be relatively constant over a long period of time, and a highly organic medium makes this impossible.

Increasing medium depth and moisture levels also makes the roof more hospitable to weeds. Hence, while many tree seedlings will not survive in a 3 in. (7.5 cm), non-irrigated system during a dry period, they will become a problem if irrigation is provided, because their roots quickly grow very large. In turn, budgetary impacts need to be made a part of the specification, recognizing that after-installation costs will be incurred for maintenance of the site and the plant material. If access to the roof is limited, maintenance costs will be even more expensive.

Research has shown that moisture, even more so than depth of substrate, determines a plant's growth patterns and survivability (Thuring 2005). Many plants will survive in shallow substrate if regular irrigation or natural moisture is present. If the client desires more diversity and the inclusion of herbaceous perennials, however, a greater medium depth and some type of irrigation system are essential.

Roof slope/pitch and drainage factors

Moderately steeply sloped roofs (3:12 to 5:12) and steeply pitched roofs (5:12 to 12:12) create significant variability in water-holding characteristics of the green roof medium. Substrate located at the lowest edge of a sloped roof will

Moderately sloped roofs, including this one (with a 3:12 pitch) on a building of the Wildlands Conservancy in Emmaus, Pennsylvania, drain more quickly than flat roofs and are prone to dryness and nutrient loss near the top of the slope.

hold large amounts of water but results in reduced air space volume. The higher up the slope, the less water is available and the more air space, because of the gravitational pull of the long water column. Plant species should be chosen in part based on these moisture differences.

Proper irrigation system design can help balance slope-based water availability differences. Sufficient pitch (0.25:12) is needed, plus an efficient drainage system, to avoid water ponding that could cause lack of sufficient oxygen for root systems and lead to root diseases. In a deeper medium, "dead flat" roofs can be accommodated by increasing the thickness and transmissivity of the drainage layer and by introducing internal collector pipes (Miller 2005). On sloped roofs, designers should work closely with plant specialists on correct placement of the plants for optimizing the system. The greater the slope, the faster it drains, thus creating very dry conditions relative to flat roofs and causing nutrients and water to be lost at a greater rate. Nutrition is most easily lost from the peak of the roof, and plant selection and maintenance should reflect that.

Plant Establishment

The key to a green roof's longevity is rapid plant establishment. If the roof is unsuccessful in the establishment phase, it will lengthen the time of the return on investment. It is cheaper in the long run to invest the necessary time and materials to ensure rapid plant establishment, even if only for the first few weeks of the installation and depending on local conditions at the time. It is also prudent to plant early enough in the season to allow plants to root in thoroughly before the first killing frost. Trials performed at Penn State University on plant establishment showed that well-established plants were much more likely to survive winter and drought than plants that were poorly established (Thuring 2005).

Plant establishment needs vary widely, but they are critical to the long-term success of the green roof. Whether the roof is planted from seeds, cuttings, or plugs, the plants are best coddled until they become acclimated to their growing conditions. This involves providing sufficient water to promote growth, especially root growth. With proper care during the establishment period, coverage will be achieved at an earlier date.

If planting occurs in spring or fall in areas where natural rainfall is regular and abundant, irrigation may not be needed. On many installations on the US East Coast, for example, plants require and receive no supplemental irrigation at all, not even upon planting. For other parts of the North American continent, such as the southwestern and southern US, plants require care until established. This may vary from daily to periodic irrigation, which can be achieved through several methods, including built-in irrigation systems, lawn sprinklers, and even garden hoses, if necessary. Irrigation needs should be ascertained and used for the specified plants, location, and time of year in which the project is installed. Replacing the entire vegetation layer of a green roof is not only costly but inefficient, and it will delay the roof's maturation.

Installation Methods

The best installation method for a given site must marry the speed at which the green roof should be fully mature to the simplicity or complexity of the design, to the budget, to the availability of resources and expertise, and to the maintenance needs and abilities of the person responsible for maintaining the site.

Seeds

As of this writing, no wholly seeded green roof installations exist in North America, but it seems likely that seeded installations will eventually appear. Market pressures to decrease installation costs are causing more thought to be given to direct sowing on green roofs, and with the proper mix of hand broadcasting and hydro-seeding equipment, direct sowing could become a viable—and the least expensive—planting method. Large-scale use of green roofs will occur only when cities commonly install hundreds of acres of green roofs, thus driving down the overall cost of green roof installation and making it cost effective to invest in dedicated hydro-seeding equipment. Contractors in North America must also find the right seed mix, the proper carrier for the seed, and climatic conditions that will make large-scale hydro-seeding possible.

Of the planting methods available, a seeded green roof takes the most time to mature—generally two to three years for coverage. Additionally, limited numbers of species can be reliably germinated on a roof, and all require some supplemental irrigation during the germination and establishment phases. Seeds are best sown in spring or fall, depending on the climate, using a propagation specialist with experience in hand sowing or hydro-seeding technology. Some plant species such as *Talinum* are self sowing, so they reestablish each growing season without the need for acquiring new seed. In areas with reliably damp climates and good germinating times, seasonal opportunities for seeding may exist, much as one would establish a lawn. However seed is broadcast, it should be mixed with some type of carrier medium, such as sand or cellulose, to ensure even application.

Seed specifications for green roofs should include rapidly germinating seed that needs no special treatment such as scarification or cold or warm storage periods. *Sedum album* is a good candidate for seeding small areas as it germinates readily, is drought hardy, and is easy to establish. *Petrorhagia* and *Dianthus* species germinate rapidly and have potential for seed propagation. To achieve full coverage of a roof in a short time period, quicker maturing annuals could be mixed with perennial seeds, although this risks the annuals overrunning the perennials.

The fact that virtually no wholly seeded green roof installations exist in North America gives reason for caution in propagating plants directly on a green roof. Therefore, seeding is best utilized for adding some color to an installation while a roof is growing in or for introducing more seasonal color onto an already established roof. Seeding also presents a challenge in delivering a precise landscape design or realistic picture of how the roof will look, unless a single species is used and weeds are controlled. For example, on a 10,000 square foot (929 square meter) green roof, where *Sedum* is specified and where two plugs per square foot are optimum, about 20 seeds per square foot are necessary to achieve even coverage. This means evenly distributing roughly a gram of material over 10,000 square feet—an extremely challenging undertaking.

Cuttings

Most plants on green roofs are installed using plugs and cuttings. Cuttings are a viable and increasingly popular method for establishing *Sedum* on green roofs and are the most commonly used method of installation in Germany. Cuttings are quicker to establish than seeds, and, depending on time of year and local weather conditions, they may not require supplemental irrigation to help them get established. Some installers do, however, thoroughly saturate the medium before planting, which allows for gradual absorption of moisture into the cuttings (Miller 2005).

Cuttings should be evenly distributed across the roof at a rate of 25 to 50 pounds per 1000 square feet (92 square meters). To ensure as much diversity and survivability as possible, several species and cultivars can be planted.

Cuttings are harvested from a mixed bed of sedums.

Cuttings are broadcast onto the prepared medium of a green roof.

This will avoid gaping holes in an installation if one type thrives more than another under certain conditions such as drought.

Cuttings, while more expensive than seeds, are cheaper than plugs, require less labor, and achieve coverage much earlier than seeds alone. They are an excellent option for clients who wish to have a well-covered roof within a year after planting, although cuttings are more fragile to ship than plugs and may require a refrigerated method of transportation to ensure their survival. Cuttings require minimal labor to broadcast, which can by done by hand. Daichi, a Japanese company that also supplies plants to North America, offers cuttings that are imbedded in biodegradable sheets for ease of installation. The sheets are rolled out and then watered.

On the downside, cuttings can limit precise design options, albeit not as much as seeds, and using cuttings effectively reduces plant choices for most green roofs to *Sedum* and *Delosperma* species. Cuttings can be used in combination with herbaceous plugs or seeds. It is impossible, however, to use cuttings from herbaceous plants for green roof purposes without first rooting them in a potted growing medium. Cuttings require between 12 to 18 months of growth for full coverage.

Plugs

Plugs, essentially cuttings with established root systems, offer a compromise between cost and flexibility. One practical benefit of plugs is that they

Plug trays await installation.

A landscaping crew removes plugs from trays in preparation for planting on the roof of the Montgomery Park building in Baltimore, Maryland.

An unplanted roof features bare medium just before planting.

lengthen the planting season from the last frost of spring to late summer and even early fall in mild climates. They also open the door for greater plant diversity, because fully rooted plugs store sufficient energy to allow for easy establishment, depending on local climate. Unlike container-grown plants, plugs are sized to the medium and are inexpensive enough to allow the plant material cost to remain low. Specifying plugs allows for the most precise and highly individualized designs of all planting methods.

Plug trays vary in size and are denoted by the number of cells in the tray, most commonly 36, 50, or 72, of which 72 is the most common size. Plugs are easily packed and shipped in boxes and can survive several days en route.

The most commonly specified rate for planting plugs is two plugs per square foot, which will provide full coverage of the roof in 12 to 18 months. Doubling the amount of plugs per square foot will reduce the time to full coverage, but will increase, if not double, the costs. Different plants have different rates of spread, which should be factored into the specifications—some plants may require more than two plugs per square foot to achieve maturity in two years.

The same roof shows how plants have established in 12 months.

Nursery containers

Nursery containers are occasionally specified for extensive green roofs when more established plants are needed from the beginning. In North America, containers vary in size from 2 to 4 in., to quarts and gallons. Where the medium is deep enough to accommodate the additional root mass of a nursery container–grown plant, vegetation will spread more quickly than that of plugs.

Rarely are container plants suitable for transplant onto green roofs, however, because they are grown in a commercial nursery medium, which is highly organic and generally unsuitable for extensive green roofs. In addition, an organic medium will shrink much more readily than an inorganic mixture, which can adversely affect plant survivability. Also, as the containers increase in size, so, too, do the plants' root masses. The typical green roof medium is not sized to accommodate the root mass of a plant grown in a quart or gallon container, and the extra weight of the plant will likely exceed the medium's ability to support it. If the medium depth in the pot is deeper than the medium depth on the roof, the root ball will need to be broken apart or shortened, partially defeating the reason for starting with a larger plant.

Container size and plant spacing also affect total system weight. The total weight of the saturated medium could exceed design specifications when transplanting from large containers. Simply put, a plant in a gallon pot does not belong in a 4 in. (10 cm) substrate. The soil around the roots of the transplants will be mixed with the soil designed for a specific maximum roof weight load. The final soil mixture should be moderately low in nutrients and organic matter, possess a neutral or slightly alkaline pH, and drain freely. Significant amounts of transplant container soil can upset the planned nutrient content, percentage of organic matter, and weight of the final planting mixture.

Other considerations aside, in most cases it is simply not economical to plant an entire roof using container-grown plants, as plants grown in quart and gallon containers are more costly than smaller sized seedlings or plugs. At most, nursery containers can be used to plant discrete areas of the roof, such as a culinary section, which might be planted in a deeper medium than the rest of the roof.

Vegetated mats

Vegetated mats are long rolls of pregrown plants set in a thin layer of mesh and medium and are fully mature upon installation. They are installed in strips on top of a base substrate, which provides eventual root support.

Vegetated mats are rolled in preparation for shipping.

The precise plant composition of mats is difficult to predict, as some plants will grow more vigorously than others, crowding and sometimes overwhelming other species. Mats are very heavy and bulky to transport, cannot be shipped long distances during hot weather months unless they are in refrigerated trucks, and may require special expertise and equipment, such as front-end loaders or cranes, to maneuver into place. In addition, mats must be ordered and grown a minimum of one year before installation (although one company, Xeroflor, offers pregrown vegetated mats in its inventory). Vegetated mats work especially well for sloped applications such as pitched roofs, because the mats are finished products and suffer virtually no loss of medium due to erosion.

Modules

Modules are discrete vegetated systems. Several companies, including Green Grid and Green Roof Blocks, offer modular systems. Modules typically consist of black plastic squares or rectangles encompassing 4 to 16 square feet (0.4 to 1.5 square meters) per unit.

Modules are the most expensive green roof planting option. They share many of the advantages and disadvantages of vegetated mats, but they include more medium, which adds to the individual weight of each module. Modules allow for greater precision and variability of design than mats, and they are more easily replaced, since they are self-contained units that can be

Newly planted modules are grown in anticipation of installation one year later.

Modules were installed on the green roof of the Center for Urban Ecology in Washington, D.C.

lifted out without great disturbance to the rest of the installation. Modules also require virtually no horticultural knowledge for installation and can be installed like pavers on a walkway or patio.

Maintenance: Weeding, Watering, and Fertilizing

With the exception of mats and modules, most extensive green roof installations take 12 to 18 months to establish. This is a critical period for green roofs, during which maintenance is paramount. Green roof success is largely achieved from the proper relationship among plant selection, climatic conditions, and medium. On the most successful green roofs, maintenance is an integral part of the installation. Hand weeding, for example, is needed more during the establishment phase than at any other time, and the long-term health and success of the green roof is impacted by the presence or absence of such care.

Some weeds are inevitable on green roofs, and throughout the life of the roof, new weeds will be introduced via wind, birds, or people. Left unchecked, they can be dangerous to the health of the roof. Weeds can choke out the specified plants during optimal growing times, consume nutrients and water, and then die during periods of drought and stress, leaving large

As installations age, moss and other invasive plants can take over due to inadequate nutrition or inappropriate pH levels.

empty patches on the roof. Once fully vegetated, green roofs are much more resistant to weed seed germination, but in the establishment stages, plenty of exposed medium is available for weed seeds to find a home. If the medium contains weed seeds from the beginning, weeds are inevitable. Hence a sterile medium should always be specified and tested prior to installation.

Weeds can become a problem for any installation that is not properly maintained, especially during the establishment phase.

Even with a sterile medium, weed seeds will be introduced; for this reason, early and regular weeding is critical. During establishment of the green roof, weeding must occur over a period of months to control the varied weed species. Weeding should always occur before the weeds set seed, so knowing the seasonal patterns of weed germination in the planting area is good practice. If weeding occurs after the weedy plants have produced viable seeds, the selected use of preemergent herbicides may also be necessary. These herbicides will not affect the established plants.

All green roofs require fertilization during the establishment phase. Because the initial medium should have sufficient fertility for the first growing season, supplemental fertilization should occur a year after planting, using slow-release fertilizers only, which reduces the amount of nitrate and phosphate runoff. The analysis most commonly used on green roofs is 14-14-14 with trace elements. Yearly applications of a slow-release fertilizer, at a rate of 5 grams of nitrogen per 1000 square feet (92 square meters), will maintain plant health and provide enough fertility to allow hardy succulents to grow, but not so much that it encourages weeds. After five or six years, fertilization may not be necessary at all or could be decreased, depending on the health of the installation.

Plant Growth Rate

Rate of growth and ultimate shoot height are important plant-selection criteria, because the fewer plants needed to fill a given roof area, the less expen-

Selection problems

Before selecting plants, several potential problems must be carefully examined: fire hazards; thorny, poisonous, or invasive plant features; medium nutrient content; salt spray and acid rain presence; and heat and wind effects on plants. In areas where brush fires are a concern, grasses and herbaceous perennials that die back should be cut back appropriately and removed or avoided altogether, because at certain times of year their shoots die and dry, making them both unsightly and flammable. Sedums and other succulents, on the other hand, store large percentages of water in their leaf tissues and can act as fire retardants. At the least, fire-retardant plants should be used to surround flammable plants to reduce potential spread of an accidental fire. Thorny seed heads or sharply pointed leaves can be hazardous to people walking on or touching the plants, so they may be unsuited to green roofs that are accessible to the public. This is equally true for species whose leaves and/or flowers are poisonous to eat or touch. Finally, because plant seed may be wind dispersed beyond the roof area, it is best to avoid seed from potentially invasive species or noxious weeds (White 2005a).

sive the installation. The best low-growing plants are 1 to 6 in. (2.5 to 15 cm) tall in flower, although plants less than 10 in. (25 cm) are acceptable. In some cases, plants can be up to 12 in. tall (30 cm) if maximum dead load allows sufficient substrate depth for deeper roots. Plants that are short at maturity are more resistant to wind damage and easier to maintain, while plants with tall stems or flower stalks are more likely to require pruning to maintain appearance and remove dried and dead plant tissue, which are fire hazards. Although dead plant tissue of some plant species easily decomposes over time, other species, such as grasses, have high fiber content and take a long time to decompose naturally. Dry biomass buildup increases the potential for fire spread.

Preparing Extensive Green Roofs for Planting

Before plants are installed, all structural and protective work on the roof should be completed. In some cases, the medium may be used for membrane protection, but it should not be planted until the trades people have finished their work on the roof to avoid potential damage to the plants. Once the roof

Planting should never take place until all other work on the site is finished, as construction materials can kill the plants and compromise a roof's integrity. Photograph by Terry McGlade.

is ready for planting, the medium can be spread to the specified depth and thoroughly moistened. If necessary, exterior grade, ¾-inch plywood pieces can be laid on top of the substrate and used for foot or wheelbarrow traffic to planting sites. Plastic film should not be laid over the substrate, because it may overheat the medium and affect plants. Before installation, the medium should be covered and kept weed free once it arrives on the building site.

Irrigation

Depending on the season, local rainfall, and other local conditions, one should assess whether or not plants need more than a single watering upon installation. If supplemental irrigation is required, which is likely in the southwestern US and in other dry regions, depending on season, plants should be kept well watered for the first three weeks after transplanting, with gradual tapering off to begin adapting plants to drier conditions.

In areas where watering is necessary, the plants will require care from a horticulturist or nursery employee who has training in proper irrigation techniques—an absolute essential for good plant establishment and growth, which is a predictor of future survivability. If an automatic irrigation system with solenoid valves and time clock or computer-activated controllers is used, less frequent attention may be necessary. However, any system should be monitored, especially during the critical first three weeks of plant establishment. One should never walk away from a newly planted project without being sure that the irrigation system is working properly and all plants have had a thorough initial watering.

Young plants tend to feature an imbalance of top growth, or shoots, to root growth. Young plants can wilt and become stressed even when the substrate has sufficient available water. During sunny and/or windy, hot, humid weather, an overhead irrigation system can be used to help cool stressed plants. This is usually necessary only during initial plant establishment. Thereafter, where needed, a sub-irrigation system is more efficient in delivering water to the root system with little or no evaporative loss. Sub-irrigation systems direct the water only to plant roots, lose less water to evaporation, and are not visible. A sub-irrigation system's drip outlets are usually on 12 to 14 in. (31 to 36 cm) square spacing and are located about an inch (3 cm) below the substrate surface. Temporary overhead sprinkler systems are often used for initial plant establishment, and then long-term irrigation is provided by a sub-irrigation system (White 2005b).

After initial plant establishment in dry areas, irrigating may be unnecessary, but the irrigation system may need to remain available in case of unusual weather patterns to avoid costly dieback because of insufficient water. A coarse, lightweight gravel mulch can be used to help reduce evaporation from the surface.

Planting Times

Best planting times vary with climate. Still, some areas and times are so favorable to plant establishment, relative to plant selection, that planting vegetation involves minimal work. In areas with moist, temperate spring climates, such as Maryland and Pennsylvania, for example, spring is an ideal time to plant, and supplemental irrigation is usually not necessary (Miller 2005). In those same areas in July and August, however, surface irrigation may be necessary for a number of days or weeks to provide enough moisture for the plants to establish successfully. Some general planting rules apply in most of North America.

In the northern US, install plants from just after the last average frost in spring until several weeks before the first average frost in fall to allow time for plants to establish. In one Michigan study, for example, the majority of the plugs planted on a green roof in September did not survive the winter because they were not yet well-established when cold weather occurred. Many were partially heaved out of the medium due to frost action (Rowe 2005).

In areas where winters are mild and moist, such as in the US Pacific Northwest, fall and winter may be a better time to introduce plants to the medium. Plants can be set out in spring or fall as long as the ground stays

Advance notice to growers for plant production

Green roof plant buyers can experience cost benefits by developing contract-growing arrangements at least six and preferably nine months before green roof plants are needed. If native species are ordered but are not normally grown in large quantities by a particular vendor, one year's advance notice may be necessary. In North America, green roof plants should be contract grown for June though October planting, allowing the commercial grower to utilize space better during the peak growing season.

warmer than 40°F (4°C) at night for at least a month. Plant in spring if normal regular rainfall will help establish young plants or germinate seed. Plant in fall when fall and winter rains and/or snow cover will provide moisture for early growth. Plant any time in the summer that adequate irrigation can be supplied and the average daytime temperature is less than 86°F (30°C).

In the US Deep South, arid Southwest, and parts of California, late fall and winter plantings survive best. Establishing a green roof in the US Southwest is a largely theoretical matter at this date, but with data gathered from green roofs in Mexico, the following general rules apply: Never plant during the dry and hot season, which runs from May through September. During the plants' establishment phase, daily irrigation is necessary to ensure viability. Because in areas of great dryness the medium is susceptible to blowing away, part of the reason for watering initially is to ensure that the medium is heavy enough to stay on the roof before the plants have established any kind of root structure. Unless the substrate is substantially deeper than 6 in. (15 cm) and is irrigated, the only plants that will survive in hot and arid areas will necessarily be succulent plants, not leafy herbaceous perennials.

CHAPTER 4

Plant Guide

THIS CHAPTER provides information about specific plants used for green roofs. Various terms are used to describe plant attributes, and a brief statement provides specific information that may be helpful in choosing plants for a project. However, one should always consult with knowledgeable growers and horticulturists for specific design questions.

In this chapter, botanical names are used rather than common names, as many of the plants either don't have common names or share common names. Synonyms are also included as appropriate, as some plants can be known and sold in the nursery trade by more than one botanical name.

Flower and foliage color are provided, along with the typical bloom times or range or times for design purposes. Actual bloom time may vary somewhat according to zone and location.

Hardiness zone information reflects the cold hardiness of each plant according to USDA established hardiness zones. If sources included slight differences regarding plant hardiness, the most conservative estimates were used—so, for example, if a plant is listed as being on the edge between zones 5 and 6, the higher hardiness zone is cited to be safe. In our experience, a building's elevation does not decrease temperatures to the point of changing an area's hardiness zone. Heat zones have been deliberately omitted, because no data is available to quantify the amount of summer heat that is added by the urban heat island effect, nor do we know how plants react to it in any quantifiable way.

Plants are divided into two broad categories: groundcovers versus accent plants. A selection of mostly groundcovers for each green roof is essential for its long-term viability. Groundcovers stabilize the medium and their cover prevents weeds from establishing. In many cases, however, groundcovers are not high in ornamental value, so accents are used to provide color, texture, and height and, in some cases, to block unsightly mechanical systems from view.

The terms *self sowing* and *not self sowing* indicate a plant's ability to self seed. Plants described as self sowing often spread to some significant degree; some can become troublesome spreaders on a green roof and on the ground below and can impact a planting design. Also noted is whether a plant produces viable seed.

Countries or regions in which the plant is a native, has naturalized, or both, are also included.

Height figures indicate the mature height of the plant as experienced in the trade. The height of plants on green roofs can be, and in many cases is, much shorter. Plants can be as much as one third their normal height under stressful conditions such as a thin medium and low fertility. Spread figures represent a plant's annual spread, not its lifetime spread. Competition from other plants can limit spread. Use this information to help determine planting density on the roof. Keep in mind that a plant's spread and height will vary according to a number of factors, especially medium depth and the availability of water and nutrients.

Planting medium requirements are also included to indicate the depth of the medium needed to sustain a plant.

Light requirements are also provided. *Full sun* indicates that the plant requires full sun for a least six hours or more per day during the growing season. *Mixed sun/shade* means that the plant requires full sun for between three and six hours per day. *Shade* means that the plant can endure shaded conditions for most of the day, most notably during the afternoon. Note that in urban settings, the amount of sun a roof receives is often impacted by the shadows from other buildings, which causes the sun to appear and disappear more often than at ground-level gardens. Because of that, a total accumulation of three hours of sunlight may actually take six hours or more, even if the roof appears to receive continuous sun. On the other hand, some roofs may receive the benefit of more sunlight, due to the reflective qualities of buildings. In addition, shade from buildings is brighter than shade from trees because of the higher reflectivity of buildings. Careful observation of the site is needed before the plants are specified.

Irrigation refers to an installed irrigation system on the green roof, not a temporary irrigation system or any hand watering that is undertaken for establishment.

Achillea millefolium (Asteraceae)

- White flowers, green foliage
- Blooms midsummer
- Hardiness zone 3
- Groundcover
- Self sowing
- Found in North America, Australia, New Zealand
- Height to 16 in. (40 cm)
- Spreads 6 in. (15 cm)
- Planting medium 6 in. (15 cm) deep
- Full sun

A widely distributed wildflower used in meadow-style green roof designs.

Achillea tomentosa (Asteraceae)

- Yellow flowers, green foliage
- Blooms midsummer
- Hardiness zone 3
- Groundcover
- Self sowing
- Found in Europe, northern Asia
- Height to 8 in. (20 cm)
- Spreads 6 in. (15 cm)
- Planting medium 6 in. (15 cm) deep
- Full sun

Similar in foliage habit to *A. millefolium*, but with a much showier bloom.

Achillea tomentosa. Photograph by Georg Uebelhart, Jelitto Perennial Seeds.

Achillea millefolium. Photograph by Georg Uebelhart, Jelitto Perennial Seeds.

Aethionema grandiflorum

(Brassicaceae)
Light pink flowers, green foliage
Blooms early summer
Hardiness zone 5
Accent
Not self sowing
Found in Southwest Asia, Mediterranean
Height to 8 in. (20 cm)
Spreads 12 in. (30 cm)
Planting medium 6 in. (15 cm) deep
Full sun

Nice mounding habit suitable for a border. Needs additional water in dry periods.

Agastache rugosa (Lamiaceae)

Blue flowers, green foliage
Blooms midsummer to midautumn
Hardiness zone 8
Accent
Not self sowing
Found in Japan, China
Height to 24 in. (60 cm)
Spreads 8 in. (20 cm)
Planting medium 6 in. (15 cm) deep
Full sun, mixed sun/shade, shade

A favorite of bees, this plant is surprisingly tough once established.

Agastache rugosa f. *albiflora*

(Lamiaceae)
White flowers, green foliage
Blooms midsummer to midautumn
Hardiness zone 9
Accent
Not self sowing
Found in Japan, China
Height to 25 in. (63 cm)
Spreads 8 in. (20 cm)
Planting medium 6 in. (15 cm) deep
Full sun, mixed sun/shade, shade

White blooms last over a long period. Tall plant is suitable for distant viewing.

Aethionema grandiflorum. Photograph by Georg Uebelhart, Jelitto Perennial Seeds.

Agastache rugosa

Agastache rupestris (Lamiaceae)
  Orange flowers, blue-green foliage
  Blooms midsummer to midautumn
  Hardiness zone 6
  Accent
  Not self sowing

Found in southwestern US
Height to 25 in. (63 cm)
Spreads 10 in. (25 cm)
Planting medium 6 in. (15 cm) deep
Full sun, mixed sun/shade

Beautiful, deep-throated flowers attract hummingbirds. Becomes somewhat shrublike with time.

Alchemilla saxatilis (Rosaceae)
  Yellow flowers, green foliage
  Blooms midsummer to midautumn
  Hardiness zone 3
  Groundcover
  Not self sowing
  Found in Europe
  Height to 6 in. (15 cm)
  Spreads 10 in. (25 cm)
  Planting medium 6 in. (15 cm) deep
  Mixed sun/shade, shade

Slow creeping groundcover.

Agastache rugosa f. *albiflora*

Agastache rupestris

Alchemilla saxatilis. Photograph by Georg Uebelhart, Jelitto Perennial Seeds.

Allium acuminatum (Alliaceae)
Purple flowers, green foliage
Blooms midsummer
Hardiness zone 7
Accent
Self sowing
Found in Pacific Northwest, Rocky
  Mountain regions
Height to 6 in. (15 cm)
Spreads 6 in. (15 cm)
Planting medium 4 in. (10 cm) deep
Full sun, mixed sun/shade

North American plant expecially suited for roofs in the western United States. Found in open rocky areas, it is often one of the first plants to return after a fire.

Allium cernuum (Alliaceae)
Rose and white flowers, green
  foliage
Blooms late summer
Hardiness zone 4
Accent
Self sowing
Found in North America
Height to 18 in. (45 cm)
Spreads 6 in. (15 cm)
Planting medium 4 in. (10 cm) deep
Full sun, mixed sun/shade

Reliable North American native. Nodding flower habit.

Allium moly (Alliaceae)
Yellow flowers, green foliage
Blooms early summer
Hardiness zone 7
Accent
Self sowing
Found in southwestern Europe
Height to 10 in. (25 cm)
Spreads 6 in. (15 cm)
Planting medium 4 in. (10 cm) deep
Full sun, mixed sun/shade

Plant as a bulb in the fall for best results. Needs more reliable mois-

Allium acuminatum. Photograph by Georg Uebelhart, Jelitto Perennial Seeds.

Allium cernuum. Photograph by Georg Uebelhart, Jelitto Perennial Seeds.

ture than other *Allium* species, so can be planted near drains.

Allium oreophilum (Alliaceae)
    Purple flowers, green foliage
    Blooms early summer
    Hardiness zone 4
    Accent
    Self sowing
    Found in central Asia
    Height to 6 in. (15 cm)
    Spreads 6 in. (15 cm)
    Planting medium 4 in. (10 cm) deep
    Full sun, mixed sun/shade

Long-lived plant is usually shipped as bulbs, but can be grown from seed. Short habit and very tough; provides early summer color.

Allium schoenoprasum (Alliaceae)
    Pink flowers, green foliage
    Blooms late spring
    Hardiness zone 4
    Accent
    Self sowing
    Found in Europe
    Height to 10 in. (25 cm)
    Spreads 6 in. (15 cm)
    Planting medium 4 in. (10 cm) deep
    Full sun, mixed sun/shade

Most common allium for green roofs; has culinary use as well.

Allium oreophilum

Allium moly. Photograph by Georg Uebelhart, Jelitto Perennial Seeds.

Allium schoenoprasum

Allium senescens subsp. *montanum* var. *glaucum* (Alliaceae)

Pink flowers, blue-green foliage

Blooms early autumn

Hardiness zone 5

Accent

Self sowing

Found in Europe to Siberia

Height to 8 in. (20 cm)

Spreads 6 in. (15 cm)

Planting medium 4 in. (10 cm) deep

Full sun, mixed sun/shade

Interesting foliage plant with spiraling blue-green leaves. Provides much needed color late in the season.

Allium tuberosum (Alliaceae)

White flowers, green foliage

Blooms late summer

Hardiness zone 7

Accent

Self sowing

Found in Southeast Asia

Height to 15 in. (38 cm)

Spreads 8 in. (20 cm)

Planting medium 4 in. (10 cm) deep

Full sun, mixed sun/shade

Garlic chives also used for culinary green roofs. Attracts butterflies. Seedlings may need to be culled or deadheaded to keep from spreading.

Alyssum montanum 'Berggold' (Brassicaceae)

Yellow flowers, green foliage

Blooms early summer

Hardiness zone 6

Groundcover

Not self sowing

Found in Europe

Height to 6 in. (15 cm)

Spreads 10 in. (25 cm)

Planting medium 6 in. (15 cm) deep

Full sun

Can be grown to 10,000 ft. (3050 m) in altitude; suitable for high green roofs in the western US, with irrigation during the dry months.

Allium senescens subsp. *montanum* var. *glaucum*. Photograph courtesy of Mary Walters, imagebotanica.com.

Allium tuberosum. Photograph by Georg Uebelhart, Jelitto Perennial Seeds.

Alyssum serpyllifolium

(Brassicaceae)
Pale yellow flowers, green foliage
Blooms early summer
Hardiness zone 8
Groundcover
Not self sowing
Found in southwestern Europe
Height to 3 in. (7 cm)
Spreads 10 in. (25 cm)
Planting medium 6 in. (15 cm) deep
Full sun

Dwarf plant is a little more drought tolerant than other *Alyssum* species. Needs well-drained medium.

Anacyclus pyrethrum var. *depressus* (Asteraceae)

White flowers with yellow centers, gray-green foliage
Blooms early summer
Hardiness zone 6
Accent
Not self sowing
Found in Spain, Morocco
Height to 4 in. (10 cm)
Spreads 8 in. (20 cm)
Planting medium 6 in. (15 cm) deep
Full sun, mixed sun/shade

Ornamental plant with gray-green foliage and red accents under the flower petals. Will not survive in hot, humid weather; use in cooler summer locations.

Alyssum montanum 'Berggold'. Photograph by Georg Uebelhart, Jelitto Perennial Seeds.

Alyssum serpyllifolium. Photograph by Georg Uebelhart, Jelitto Perennial Seeds.

Anacyclus pyrethrum var. *depressus.* Photograph by Georg Uebelhart, Jelitto Perennial Seeds.

Antennaria dioica (Asteraceae)

Pink flowers, gray foliage
Blooms late spring
Hardiness zone 5
Groundcover
Not self sowing
Found in North America
Height to 4 in. (10 cm)
Spreads 8 in. (20 cm)
Planting medium 4 in. (10 cm) deep
Full sun, mixed sun/shade

Flowers don't open fully; more attractive in bud. Stoloniferous nature; may creep around the roof. Use with *A. neglecta* for a US West Coast native planting.

Antennaria plantaginifolia

(Asteraceae)
White flowers with pink tinges, green foliage
Blooms late spring

Hardiness zone 3
Groundcover
Not self sowing
Found in North American upper
  Great Plains
Height to 10 in. (25 cm)
Spreads 8 in. (20 cm)
Planting medium 4 in. (10 cm) deep
Full sun, mixed sun/shade

Tough little groundcover with much wider leaves than most *Antennaria*. Prefers good drainage.

Anthemis tinctoria (Asteraceae)

Yellow flowers, green foliage
Blooms midsummer
Hardiness zone 6
Accent
Self sowing
Found in southern Europe
Height to 19 in. (48 cm)
Spreads 10 in. (25 cm)
Planting medium 6 in. (15 cm) deep
Full sun

Commonly used on German green roofs. Can be weedy. Will not survive long dry periods.

Antennaria dioica. Photograph by Georg Uebelhart, Jelitto Perennial Seeds.

Antennaria plantaginifolia

Anthyllis vulneraria

(Papilionaceae)

Yellow/orange flowers, green foliage

Blooms early summer

Hardiness zone 7

Accent

Not self sowing

Found in the Alps, Pyrenees

Height to 6 in. (15 cm)

Spreads 6 in. (15 cm)

Planting medium 6 in. (15 cm) deep

Full sun, mixed sun/shade

Likes the low fertility of green roofs and is used in many herbal medicines, hence the common name kidney vetch. Interesting plant for a hospital green roof.

Aquilegia canadensis 'Little Lanterns' (Ranunculaceae)

Red flowers with yellow centers, green foliage

Blooms early spring to midspring

Hardiness zone 3

Accent

Self sowing

Found in North America

Height to 10 in. (25 cm)

Spreads 8 in (20 cm)

Planting medium 6 in. (15 cm) deep

Mixed sun/shade, shade

Shorter selection of *A. canadensis*. May not survive in times of drought.

Anthemis tinctoria. Photograph by Georg Uebelhart, Jelitto Perennial Seeds.

Anthyllis vulneraria. Photograph by Georg Uebelhart, Jelitto Perennial Seeds.

Aquilegia canadensis 'Little Lanterns'. Photograph by Georg Uebelhart, Jelitto Perennial Seeds.

Arenaria montana

(Caryophyllaceae)
White flowers with yellow centers,
   green foliage
Blooms midspring to midsummer
Hardiness zone 4
Accent
Not self sowing
Found in Portugal, France
Height to 4 in. (10 cm)
Spreads 20 in. (50 cm)
Planting medium 6 in. (15 cm) deep
Full sun, mixed sun/shade

Plant familiar to rock gardeners;
can be used on green roofs to create
a mounding effect.

Armeria maritima

(Plumbaginaceae)
Pink flowers, green foliage
Blooms midspring

Hardiness zone 4
Accent
Not self sowing
Found on coastlines of Europe,
   Chile, US Pacific Northwest
Height to 6 in. (15 cm)
Spreads 6 in. (15 cm)
Planting medium 6 in. (15 cm) deep
Mixed sun/shade

Salt tolerant; good choice for green
roofs that receive ocean spray.

Armeria maritima 'Alba'

(Plumbaginaceae)
White flowers, green foliage
Blooms midspring
Hardiness zone 4
Accent
Not self sowing
Found on coastlines of Europe,
   Chile, US Pacific Northwest
Height to 6 in. (15 cm)
Spreads 6 in. (15 cm)
Planting medium 6 in. (15 cm) deep
Mixed sun/shade

Arenaria montana. Photograph by Georg
Uebelhart, Jelitto Perennial Seeds.

Armeria maritima. Photograph by Georg
Uebelhart, Jelitto Perennial Seeds.

Stunning white blooms; can be placed for a late afternoon show of light.

Artemisia ludoviciana

(Asteraceae)
Yellow flowers, gray foliage
Blooms late summer
Hardiness zone 5
Accent
Not self sowing
Found in western US
Height to 22 in. (55 cm)
Spreads 10 in. (25 cm)
Planting medium 6 in. (15 cm) deep
Full sun

Uninteresting flowers, but good foliage. Shrublike in nature when mature.

Artemisia stelleriana

(Asteraceae)
Yellow flowers, gray foliage
Blooms late summer
Hardiness zone 4

Groundcover
Not self sowing
Found in Japan
Height to 20 in. (50 cm)
Spreads 10 in. (25 cm)
Planting medium 6 in. (15 cm) deep
Full sun

Dusty gray foliage; plant may suffer in high summer humidity.

Armeria maritima 'Alba'

Artemisia ludoviciana

Artemisia stelleriana

Aster alpinus (Asteraceae)

Light purple flowers with yellow
centers, green foliage
Blooms spring
Hardiness zone 3
Accent
Not self sowing
Found in western North America,
European mountains, western
and central Asia
Height to 9 in. (22 cm)
Spreads 6 in. (15 cm)
Planting medium 6 in. (15 cm) deep
Full sun, mixed sun/shade

Stunning flower; used with grasses
on Swarthmore College (Pennsylvania) dormitory roof.

Aster alpinus 'Dunkle Schöne'
(Asteraceae)

Purple flowers with yellow centers,
green foliage
Blooms spring
Hardiness zone 3
Accent
Not self sowing
Found in western North America,
European mountains, western
and central Asia
Height to 9 in. (22 cm)
Spreads 6 in. (15 cm)
Planting medium 6 in. (15 cm) deep
Full sun, mixed sun/shade

A darker purple cultivar of *A. alpinus*.

Aster oblongifolius (Asteraceae)

Blue-purple flowers, green foliage
Blooms early autumn to mid
autumn
Hardiness zone 5
Accent
Not self sowing
Found in eastern to north-central US
Height to 30 in. (76 cm)
Spreads 15 in. (38 cm)

Aster alpinus. Photograph by Georg Uebelhart, Jelitto Perennial Seeds.

Aster alpinus 'Dunkle Schöne'. Photograph by Georg Uebelhart, Jelitto Perennial Seeds.

Planting medium 6 in. (15 cm) deep
Full sun, mixed sun/shade

More compact, fall-blooming aster. Aromatic and showy. 'October

Skies' and 'Raydon's Favorite' are two good cultivars.

Aurinia saxatilis 'Compacta' (syn. *Alyssum saxatile* 'Compactum') (Brassicaceae)

Yellow flowers, green foliage
Blooms early summer
Hardiness zone 3
Not self sowing
Groundcover
Found in central to southeastern Europe
Height to 6 in. (15 cm)
Spreads 10 in. (25 cm)
Planting medium 6 in. (15 cm) deep
Full sun

Very floriferous, sweetly scented flower; trailing habit makes it useful for hanging over an edge.

Aster oblongifolius. Photograph by Becky Long, North Creek Nurseries.

Aurinia saxatilis 'Compacta'. Photograph by Georg Uebelhart, Jelitto Perennial Seeds.

Bouteloua curtipendula

(Poaceae)

Brown to pale purple flowers, blue-green foliage

Blooms early summer

Hardiness zone 4

Accent

Self sowing

Found in North and South America

Height to 30 in. (76 cm)

Spreads 20 in. (50 cm)

Planting medium 6 in. (15 cm) deep

Full sun, mixed sun/shade

Drought-tolerant grass from the plains; better long-term success if planted in mounded medium and cared for until established.

Bouteloua gracilis (Poaceae)

Light brown flowers, green foliage

Blooms midsummer

Hardiness zone 4

Accent

Self sowing

Found in southern and western US, Mexico

Height to 12 in. (30 cm)

Spreads 12 in. (30 cm)

Planting medium 6 in. (15 cm) deep

Full sun, mixed sun/shade

Seeds grow on one side of the flower stem. Can be established as a meadow and mowed.

Buchloe dactyloides (Poaceae)

Light brown flowers, green foliage

Blooms midsummer to midautumn

Hardiness zone 4

Groundcover

Self sowing

Found in North America

Height to 8 in. (20 cm)

Spreads 12 in. (30 cm)

Planting medium 10 in. (25 cm) deep

Full sun, mixed sun/shade

Bouteloua curtipendula

Bouteloua gracilis. Photograph by Georg Uebelhart, Jelitto Perennial Seeds.

Able to withstand foot traffic; used at ground level as a no-mow lawn. Better in climates with snow cover.

Bulbine frutescens

   (Asphodelaceae)
   Yellow flowers, green foliage
   Blooms midsummer to midautumn
   Hardiness zone 9
   Groundcover
   Not self sowing
   Found in South Africa
   Height to 8 in. (20 cm)
   Spreads 8 in. (20 cm)
   Planting medium 6 in. (15 cm) deep
   Full sun

Similar to aloe. Used medicinally for burns and rashes. Good on sub-tropical green roofs.

Calluna vulgaris (Ericaceae)
   Pink-purple flowers, green foliage
   Blooms late summer

Hardiness zone 4
Accent
Not self sowing
Found in western North America,
   Azores, northern and western
   Europe to Siberia
Height to 12 in. (30 cm)
Spreads 10 in. (25 cm)
Planting medium 6 in. (15 cm) deep
Full sun, mixed sun/shade

Semi-shrub habit when mature. Needs reliable water and good drainage.

Bulbine frutescens

Buchloe dactyloides. Photograph by Georg Uebelhart, Jelitto Perennial Seeds.

Calluna vulgaris. Photograph by Georg Uebelhart, Jelitto Perennial Seeds.

Campanula rotundifolia

(Campanulaceae)
Blue flowers, green foliage
Blooms early summer
Hardiness zone 3
Accent
Not self sowing
Found in Europe, Siberia, North
    America
Height to 12 in. (30 cm)
Spreads 8 in. (20 cm)
Planting medium 6 in. (15 cm) deep
Full sun, mixed sun/shade

Commonly used as accent on European green roofs. Will produce viable seed, but won't become a pest. Also use *C. carpatica*, *C. cochlearifolia*, and *C. poscharskyana*.

Carex flacca (Cyperaceae)

Brown flowers, blue-green foliage
Blooms late spring
Hardiness zone 5
Accent
Not self sowing
Found in Europe
Height to 8 in. (20 cm)
Spreads 8 in. (20 cm)
Planting medium 6 in. (15 cm) deep
Mixed sun/shade, shade

Semi-evergreen grass can tolerate some salt spray. No significant flower presence.

Carex humilis 'Hexe'

(Cyperaceae)
Brown flowers, green foliage
Blooms late spring
Hardiness zone 4
Accent
Not self sowing
Found in Europe to East Asia
Height to 6 in. (15 cm)
Spreads 8 in. (20 cm)
Planting medium 6 in. (15 cm) deep
Mixed sun/shade, shade

Plant forms an almost evergreen mat over time.

Campanula rotundifolia

Carex flacca

Cerastium tomentosum var. *columnae* 'Silberteppich'

(Caryophyllaceae)
White flowers, gray foliage
Blooms late spring
Hardiness zone 4
Groundcover
Not self sowing
Found in Europe, mountains of
    western Asia
Height to 6 in. (15 cm)
Spreads 12 in. (30 cm)
Planting medium 6 in. (15 cm) deep
Full sun

Abundant white flowers. Can be used to hang over edges.

Chrysopsis mariana

(Asteraceae)
Yellow flowers, green foliage
Blooms early autumn to midautumn
Hardiness zone 4
Accent
Not self sowing
Found in New York to Florida and
    west to Texas
Height to 24 in. (60 cm)
Spreads 12 in. (30 cm)
Planting medium 6 in. (15 cm) deep
Full sun

US native with late yellow bloom. Water to establish.

Cerastium tomentosum var. *columnae* 'Silberteppich'

Carex humilis 'Hexe'

Chrysopsis mariana. Photograph by Becky Long, North Creek Nurseries.

Crassula muscosa
  (Crassulaceae)
  Yellow flowers, green foliage
  Blooms late summer
  Hardiness zone 9
  Groundcover
  Not self sowing
  Found in South Africa
  Height to 30 in. (76 cm)
  Spreads 8 in. (20 cm)

Planting medium 4 in. (10 cm) deep
Full sun

Tough plant easily established by cuttings. Insignificant bloom.

Delosperma aberdeenense
  (Aizoaceae)
  Pink flowers, green foliage
  Blooms midsummer to midautumn
  Hardiness zone 8
  Groundcover
  Not self sowing
  Found in South Africa
  Height to 4 in. (10 cm)
  Spreads 8 in. (20 cm)
  Planting medium 4 in. (10 cm) deep
  Full sun

Everblooming mounding succulent. Like all *Delosperma*, dislikes winter wet even more than cold.

Delosperma aberdeenense
  'Abbey Rose' (Aizoaceae)
  Rose-pink flowers, green foliage

Crassula muscosa

Delosperma aberdeenense

Delosperma aberdeenense 'Abbey Rose'

Blooms midsummer to midautumn
Hardiness zone 8
Groundcover
Not self sowing
Found in South Africa
Height to 4 in. (10 cm)
Spreads 8 in. (20 cm)
Planting medium 4 in. (10 cm) deep
Full sun

Everblooming pink mounds; similar to *D.* 'Beaufort West'.

Delosperma aberdeenense 'Abbey White' (Aizoaceae)

White flowers, green foliage
Blooms midsummer to midautumn
Hardiness zone 8
Groundcover
Not self sowing
Found in South Africa
Height to 4 in. (10 cm)
Spreads 8 in. (20 cm)

Planting medium 4 in. (10 cm) deep
Full sun

Small white flowers cover the foliage. Also use *D. herbeum* or *D.* 'Ousberg'.

Delosperma basuticum 'Gold Nugget' (Aizoaceae)

Yellow flowers, green foliage
Blooms late spring
Hardiness zone 6
Accent
Not self sowing
Found in South Africa
Height to 2 in. (5 cm)
Spreads 4 in. (10 cm)
Planting medium 4 in. (10 cm) deep
Full sun

Species formerly known as *D. congestum*. Amazing yellow flowers totally obscure the foliage during late spring. May rebloom later in some years.

Delosperma aberdeenense 'Abbey White'

Delosperma basuticum 'Gold Nugget'

Delosperma basuticum 'White Nugget' (Aizoaceae)

White flowers with yellow centers, green foliage
Blooms late spring
Hardiness zone 6
Accent
Not self sowing
Found in South Africa
Height to 2 in. (5 cm)
Spreads 4 in. (10 cm)
Planting medium 4 in. (10 cm) deep
Full sun

Delosperma basuticum 'White Nugget'

Delosperma brunnthaleri

White-flowering plant from Denver Botanic Gardens.

Delosperma brunnthaleri (Aizoaceae)

Light yellow flowers, green foliage
Blooms midsummer to midautumn
Hardiness zone 8
Groundcover
Not self sowing
Found in South Africa
Height to 8 in. (20 cm)
Spreads 8 in. (20 cm)
Planting medium 4 in. (10 cm) deep
Full sun

Small but everblooming yellow flowers; semi-shrub habit.

Delosperma cooperi (Aizoaceae)

Pink flowers, green foliage
Blooms midsummer to midautumn
Hardiness zone 6
Groundcover
Not self sowing
Found in South Africa
Height to 4 in. (10 cm)
Spreads 12 in. (30 cm)
Planting medium 4 in. (10 cm) deep
Full sun

Most common *Delosperma* in the trade. Rapid growth with large flowers.

Delosperma dyeri (Aizoaceae)

Red flowers with light centers, green foliage
Blooms midsummer to midautumn
Hardiness zone 6
Groundcover

Not self sowing

Found in South Africa

Height to 3 in. (7 cm)

Spreads 6 in. (15 cm)

Planting medium 4 in. (10 cm) deep

Full sun

Stunning flower color that fades with sunlight, resulting in multiple shades of red.

Delosperma ecklonis var. *latifolia* (Aizoaceae)

Pink-purple flowers, green foliage

Blooms midsummer to mid-autumn

Hardiness zone 6

Groundcover

Not self sowing

Found in South Africa

Height to 4 in. (10 cm)

Spreads 10 in. (25 cm)

Planting medium 4 in. (10 cm) deep

Full sun

Reliably hardy, with rapid coverage. Can be used to hang over an edge.

Delosperma dyeri

Delosperma cooperi

Delosperma ecklonis var. *latifolia*

Delosperma 'Kelaidis'

(Aizoaceae)
Salmon-colored flowers, green
  foliage
Blooms midsummer to midautumn
Hardiness zone 6

Delosperma 'Kelaidis

Groundcover
Not self sowing
Found in South Africa
Height to 4 in. (10 cm)
Spreads 12 in. (30 cm)
Planting medium 4 in. (10 cm) deep
Full sun

Named for Denver Botanic Gardens curator Panayoti Kelaidis and patented by Plant Select. Unusual flower color, with rapid growth.

Delosperma nubigenum

'Basutoland' (Aizoaceae)
Yellow flowers, green foliage
Blooms late spring
Hardiness zone 5
Groundcover
Not self sowing
Found in South Africa
Height to 3 in. (7 cm)
Spreads 12 in. (30 cm)
Planting medium 4 in. (10 cm) deep
Full sun

Most cold hardy of the delospermas. Blooms only in spring; foliage turns pink in cold weather.

Delosperma sutherlandii

(Aizoaceae)
Dark pink flowers with yellow
  centers, green foliage
Blooms midsummer to midautumn
Hardiness zone 9
Groundcover
Not widely self sowing
Found in South Africa
Height to 3 in. (7 cm)
Spreads 6 in. (15 cm)

Delosperma nubigenum 'Basutoland'

Planting medium 4 in. (10 cm) deep
Full sun

Compact habit; produces seedlings around the parent plants.

Delosperma sutherlandii 'Peach Star' (Aizoaceae)

Peach-colored flowers with light center, green foliage
Blooms midsummer to midautumn
Hardiness zone 9
Groundcover
Not self sowing
Found in South Africa
Height to 3 in. (7 cm)
Spreads 6 in. (15 cm)
Planting medium 4 in. (10 cm) deep
Full sun

From Jelitto Perennial Seeds. Unique color true from seed.

Delosperma 'Tiffendell Magenta' (Aizoaceae)

Magenta flowers, green foliage
Blooms midsummer to midautumn
Hardiness zone 7
Groundcover
Not self sowing
Found in South Africa
Height to 4 in. (10 cm)
Spreads 8 in. (20 cm)
Planting medium 4 in. (10 cm) deep
Full sun

Great compact groundcover doesn't get leggy and blooms are close together.

Delosperma sutherlandii

Delosperma sutherlandii 'Peach Star'

Delosperma 'Tiffendell Magenta'

Deschampsia flexuosa (Poaceae)
Light brown flowers, green foliage
Blooms midsummer
Hardiness zone 5
Accent
Self sowing
Found in North America
Height to 20 in. (50 cm)
Spreads 10 in. (25 cm)
Planting medium 6 in. (15 cm) deep
Mixed sun/shade, shade

Reflective inflorescences give it a presence in morning and evening light. Needs irrigation and some shade.

Dianthus alpinus
(Caryophyllaceae)
Pink flowers, bright green foliage
Blooms early summer

Hardiness zone 4
Accent
Not self sowing
Found in eastern Alps
Height to 6 in. (15 cm)
Spreads 10 in. (25 cm)
Planting medium 6 in. (15 cm) deep
Full sun

Compact plant with scented flowers that attract bees and butterflies.

Dianthus arenarius
(Caryophyllaceae)
White flowers, green foliage
Blooms spring to summer
Hardiness zone 5
Accent
Not self sowing
Found in southern Sweden, eastern Germany, Russia to Ukraine
Height to 18 in. (45 cm)
Spreads 10 in. (25 cm)
Planting medium 6 in. (15 cm) deep
Full sun

Deschampsia flexuosa. Photograph by Georg Uebelhart, Jelitto Perennial Seeds.

Dianthus alpinus. Photograph by Georg Uebelhart, Jelitto Perennial Seeds.

Feathery white flowers with a long bloom period.

Dianthus deltoides 'Brilliant'
(Caryophyllaceae)
Bright red flowers, green foliage
Blooms early summer
Hardiness zone 3
Accent
Not self sowing
Found in Europe, northeastern US
Height to 8 in. (20 cm)
Spreads 12 in. (30 cm)
Planting medium 6 in. (15 cm) deep
Full sun

Bright blooms. Many other *D. deltoides* colors available. Not long lived on the roof.

Dianthus knappii
(Caryophyllaceae)
Pale yellow flowers, green foliage
Blooms midsummer
Hardiness zone 3
Accent
Not self sowing
Found in western Balkans
Height to 13 in. (33 cm)
Spreads 8 in. (20 cm)
Planting medium 6 in. (15 cm) deep
Full sun

Butter yellow flowers on delicate stems. Only yellow wild dianthus.

Dianthus deltoides 'Brilliant'

Dianthus arenarius

Dianthus knappii. Photograph by Georg Uebelhart, Jelitto Perennial Seeds.

Dianthus myrtinervius

(Caryophyllaceae)
Pink flowers, green foliage
Blooms late spring
Hardiness zone 7
Accent
Not self sowing
Found in Greece, Balkans
Height to 4 in. (10 cm)
Spreads 8 in. (20 cm)
Planting medium 6 in. (15 cm) deep
Full sun

Likes poor soils. Can withstand drought better than other dianthus.

Dianthus spiculifolius

(Caryophyllaceae)
White flowers with red eye, green foliage
Blooms late spring
Hardiness zone 6
Accent
Not self sowing
Found in the eastern Carpathians
Height to 6 in. (15 cm)
Spreads 8 in. (20 cm)
Planting medium 6 in. (15 cm) deep
Full sun

Nice fragrance, with dense foliage.

Dracocephalum ruyschiana

(Lamiaceae)
Blue flowers, green foliage
Blooms early summer
Hardiness zone 3
Accent
Not self sowing
Found in central Europe, Russia
Height to 10 in. (25 cm)
Spreads 6 in. (15 cm)
Planting medium 6 in. (15 cm) deep
Full sun, mixed sun/shade

Rock garden plant with hooded deep blue flowers; best viewed close up in an accessible rooftop garden.

Dianthus myrtinervius. Photograph by Georg Uebelhart, Jelitto Perennial Seeds.

Dianthus spiculifolius. Photograph by Georg Uebelhart, Jelitto Perennial Seeds.

Echium russicum (Boraginaceae)

Dark red flowers, green foliage

Blooms early to late summer

Hardiness zone 6

Accent

Not self sowing

Found in Europe, Africa, western Asia

Height to 23 in. (58 cm)

Spreads 8 in. (20 cm)

Planting medium 6 in. (15 cm) deep

Full sun

Tall red spikes and long bloom time make this a good plant for a border.

Echium vulgare (Boraginaceae)

Blue flowers, green foliage

Blooms early summer

Hardiness zone 3

Accent

Not self sowing

Found in Europe, Africa, western Asia

Height to 30 in. (76 cm)

Spreads 8 in. (20 cm)

Planting medium 6 in. (15 cm) deep

Full sun

Introduced to America from Europe in colonial times. Small thorns on the stems.

Echium vulgare. Photograph by Georg Uebelhart, Jelitto Perennial Seeds.

Dracocephalum ruyschiana. Photograph by Georg Uebelhart, Jelitto Perennial Seeds.

Echium russicum. Photograph by Georg Uebelhart, Jelitto Perennial Seeds.

Erigeron glaucus (Asteraceae)

Blue flowers with yellow centers,
  green foliage
Blooms early summer
Hardiness zone 3
Accent
Not self sowing
Found in North America
Height to 8 in. (20 cm)
Spreads 10 in. (25 cm)
Planting medium 6 in. (15 cm) deep
Full sun

Seaside, salt-tolerant plant common in the US Pacific Northwest.

Erigeron glaucus 'Albus'

(Asteraceae)
White flowers with yellow centers,
  green foliage
Blooms early summer
Hardiness zone 3
Accent
Not self sowing
Found in North America
Height to 8 in. (20 cm)
Spreads 10 in. (25 cm)
Planting medium 6 in. (15 cm) deep
Full sun

Big showy white flowers. Salt-tolerant. Needs water during dry periods.

Erigeron linearis (Asteraceae)

Yellow flowers, green foliage
Blooms early summer
Hardiness zone 4
Accent
Not self sowing
Found in North America
Height to 6 in. (15 cm)
Spreads 10 in. (25 cm)
Planting medium 6 in. (15 cm) deep
Full sun

Clump-forming native does well at higher elevations. Likes well-drained medium.

Erigeron glaucus. Photograph by Georg Uebelhart, Jelitto Perennial Seeds.

Erigeron glaucus 'Albus. Photograph by Georg Uebelhart, Jelitto Perennial Seeds.

Eriogonum flavum (Polygonaceae)

> White flowers with yellow centers, green foliage
> Blooms early summer
> Hardiness zone 7
> Accent
> Not self sowing
> Found in western North America
> Height to 10 in. (25 cm)
> Spreads 8 in. (20 cm)
> Planting medium 6 in. (15 cm) deep
> Full sun

Erigeron linearis. Photograph by Georg Uebelhart, Jelitto Perennial Seeds.

Eriogonum flavum. Photograph by Georg Uebelhart, Jelitto Perennial Seeds.

Found in the Badlands and dry valleys of North and South Dakota. Suitable for native green roofs of the northern plains.

Eriophyllum lanatum (Asteraceae)

> Yellow flowers, green foliage
> Blooms early summer
> Hardiness zone 5
> Groundcover
> Not self sowing
> Found in western US and Canada
> Height to 10 in. (25 cm)
> Spreads 20 in. (50 cm)
> Planting medium 6 in. (15 cm) deep
> Mixed sun/shade

Western native with great show of yellow flowers. Needs irrigation in dry summers.

Eriophyllum lanatum. Photograph by Georg Uebelhart, Jelitto Perennial Seeds.

Euphorbia myrsinites
(Euphorbiaceae)
Yellow flowers, blue-green foliage
Blooms late spring
Hardiness zone 6
Accent
Self sowing
Found in Mediterranean
Height to 10 in. (25 cm)
Spreads 10 in. (25 cm)
Planting medium 6 in. (15 cm) deep
Full sun

Nice foliage and structure. Can spread and may need to be controlled by weeding.

Festuca idahoensis (Poaceae)
Silver-blue flowers, blue-green foliage
Blooms late spring
Hardiness zone 6
Accent
Self sowing
Found in western US
Height to 12 in. (30 cm)
Spreads 8 in. (20 cm)
Planting medium 6 in. (15 cm) deep
Mixed sun/shade

Can be used in mass plantings, but may need to be divided or replanted over time.

Fragaria chiloensis (Rosaceae)
White flowers, green foliage
Blooms late spring
Hardiness zone 6
Accent
Not self sowing
Found in western US, South America
Height to 8 in. (20 cm)
Spreads 10 in. (25 cm)
Planting medium 6 in. (15 cm) deep
Full sun, mixed sun/shade

Wild strawberry with edible fruit. Can be used to attract birds in habitat creation.

Euphorbia myrsinites. Photograph by Georg Uebelhart, Jelitto Perennial Seeds.

Festuca idahoensis. Photograph by Angela Desaulniers, N.A.T.S. Nursery.

Galium verum (Rubiaceae)

Yellow flowers, green foliage

Blooms late spring to early autumn

Hardiness zone 3

Accent

Not self sowing

Found in North America, Europe, Asia

Height to 12 in. (30 cm)

Spreads 8 in. (20 cm)

Planting medium 6 in. (15 cm) deep

Full sun, mixed sun/shade

Attractive to more than 15 species of moths; good plant for habitat creation.

Goniolimon incanum (syn. *G. speciosum*) (Plumbaginaceae)

Pink flowers, green foliage

Blooms late summer

Hardiness zone 4

Accent

Not self sowing

Found from Turkey to Siberia

Height to 12 in. (30 cm)

Spreads 10 in. (25 cm)

Planting medium 6 in. (15 cm) deep

Full sun, mixed sun/shade

Small plant with spray of pink flowers.

Fragaria chiloensis. Photograph by Rod Nats.

Galium verum. Photograph by Georg Uebelhart, Jelitto Perennial Seeds.

Goniolimon incanum. Photograph by Georg Uebelhart, Jelitto Perennial Seeds.

Herniaria glabra (Illecebraceae)
White flowers, green foliage
Blooms late summer
Hardiness zone 5
Groundcover
Not self sowing
Found in Europe, North Africa
Height to 2 in. (5 cm)
Spreads 10 in. (25 cm)
Planting medium 6 in. (15 cm) deep
Full sun, mixed sun/shade

More drought-tolerant than thyme; rarely flowers. Can be used to hang over an edge.

Hieracium alpinum (Asteraceae)
Yellow flowers, green foliage
Blooms late summer
Hardiness zone 3
Groundcover
Self sowing
Found in northern and central
  Europe, northern Asia, eastern
  North America
Height to 8 in. (20 cm)
Spreads 8 in. (20 cm)
Planting medium 6 in. (15 cm) deep
Full sun

Compact habit, but like all *Hieracium*, will self seed throughout the roof. Best used for meadowlike plantings.

Hieracium aurantiacum (syn. *Pilosella aurantiaca*)
(Asteraceae)
Orange flowers, hairy green foliage
Blooms early to late summer
Hardiness zone 5
Groundcover
Self sowing
Found in Europe
Height to 8 in. (20 cm)
Spreads 8 in. (20 cm)
Planting medium 6 in. (15 cm) deep
Full sun

Vibrant orange flowers atop thin stems can bloom into the fall. Deadheading is required to keep it from spreading over the roof.

Herniaria glabra

Hieracium alpinum. Photograph by Georg Uebelhart, Jelitto Perennial Seeds.

Hieracium lanatum (Asteraceae)
  Yellow flowers, sliver foliage
  Blooms early to late summer
  Hardiness zone 7
  Groundcover
  Self sowing
  Found in Alps
  Height to 12 in. (30 cm)
  Spreads 8 in. (20 cm)
  Planting medium 6 in. (15 cm) deep
  Full sun

Feltlike or hairy silver foliage con-

Hieracium aurantiacum

Hieracium lanatum

trasts with yellow flowers; striking from a distance.

Hieracium pilosella (syn. *Pilosella officinarum*)
  (Asteraceae)
  Pale yellow flowers, hairy green
    foliage
  Blooms early to late summer
  Hardiness zone 6
  Groundcover
  Self sowing
  Found in Europe, northwest Siberia,
    Asia Minor
  Height to 12 in. (30 cm)
  Spreads 8 in. (20 cm)
  Planting medium 6 in. (15 cm) deep
  Full sun

Most vigorous of the *Hieracium*, forms a tight mat and spreads by seed and stolons.

Hieracium pilosella

Hieracium spilophaeum 'Leopard' (Asteraceae)

Yellow flowers, green foliage with
   purple-brown mottling
Blooms early to late summer
Hardiness zone 6
Groundcover
Self sowing
Found in western and central
   Europe
Height to 10 in. (25 cm)
Spreads 8 in. (20 cm)
Planting medium 6 in. (15 cm) deep
Full sun

Colorful variegation provides more visual interest than other *Hieracium* outside the bloom period.

Hieracium villosum (Asteraceae)

Yellow flowers, hairy green foliage
Blooms early to late summer
Hardiness zone 6
Groundcover
Self sowing
Found in the French-Swiss Jura
   Mountains, Carpathians, Alps,
   Apennines
Height to 12 in. (30 cm)
Spreads 8 in. (20 cm)
Planting medium 6 in. (15 cm) deep
Full sun

Very hairy leaves distinguish it from other *Hieracium*; attractive when covered with morning dew.

Iris humilis (syn. *I. arenaria*) (Iridaceae)

Yellow flowers, green foliage
Blooms midspring
Hardiness zone 5
Accent
Not self sowing
Found in Europe, Russia
Height to 6 in. (15 cm)
Spreads 6 in. (15 cm)
Planting medium 6 in. (15 cm) deep
Full sun, mixed sun/shade

Yellow flowers. Needs a dry period after flowering.

Hieracium spilophaeum 'Leopard'

Hieracium villosum. Photograph by Georg Uebelhart, Jelitto Perennial Seeds.

Iris pumila (Iridaceae)
  Blue-purple flowers, green foliage
  Blooms midspring
  Hardiness zone 5
  Accent
  Not self sowing

Found in eastern Europe
Height to 8 in. (20 cm)
Spreads 6 in. (15 cm)
Planting medium 6 in. (15 cm) deep
Full sun, mixed sun/shade

Good dwarf flower. Seedlings can be yellow or purple. *I. cristata* can also be used.

Iris humilis. Photograph by Georg Uebelhart, Jelitto Perennial Seeds.

Jovibarba allionii (Crassulaceae)
  White-flowers with a tinge of yellow, yellow-green foliage
  Blooms early summer
  Hardiness zone 5
  Accent
  Not self sowing
  Found in eastern Alps, Hungary, Albania
  Height to 4 in. (10 cm)
  Spreads 4 in. (10 cm)
  Planting medium 4 in. (10 cm) deep
  Full sun

Spherical in dormancy, plants will detach and roll on sloped roofs to establish in other areas. Foliage turns russet color in cold weather.

Iris pumila. Photograph by Georg Uebelhart, Jelitto Perennial Seeds.

Jovibarba allionii

Jovibarba 'Emerald Spring'

(Crassulaceae)

White flowers with pale yellow and greenish tinges, green foliage

Blooms early summer

Hardiness zone 5

Accent

Not self sowing

Found in eastern Alps

Height to 4 in. (10 cm)

Spreads 4 in. (10 cm)

Planting medium 4 in. (10 cm) deep

Full sun

Forms a mat of mounded plants that turn red in the winter; tougher than *Sempervivum*.

Kalanchoe thyrsiflora

(Crassulaceae)

Pink flowers, blue-gray foliage with red edging

Blooms late summer

Hardiness zone 9

Accent

Not self sowing

Found in South Africa

Height to 18 in. (45 cm)

Spreads 10 in. (25 cm)

Planting medium 4 in. (10 cm) deep

Full sun

In North America, use on south-facing roofs that get no frost or as an annual on roofs in cold climates.

Koeleria glauca (Poaceae)

Green to slivery flowers, blue-green foliage

Blooms early summer

Hardiness zone 4

Accent

Not self sowing

Found in central Europe, Siberia

Height to 10 in. (25 cm)

Spreads 8 in. (20 cm)

Planting medium 6 in. (15 cm) deep

Mixed sun/shade

Tough and small blue-green grass; doesn't need deadheading after flowering.

Jovibarba 'Emerald Spring'

Kalanchoe thyrsiflora

Koeleria macrantha (syn. K. pyramidata) (Poaceae)

Light green flowers, green foliage

Blooms early summer

Hardiness zone 2

Accent

Not self sowing

Found in Europe, Asia, North America

Height to 8 in. (20 cm)

Spreads 8 in. (20 cm)

Planting medium 6 in. (15 cm) deep

Mixed sun/shade

Short, clumping grass; rare in some mid-Atlantic states. Rare in the wild, so good for habitat restoration.

Lavandula angustifolia 'Hidcote Superior' (Lamiaceae)

Purple-blue flowers, gray-green foliage

Blooms late summer

Hardiness zone 5

Accent

Not self sowing

Found in Mediterranean, North Africa, western Asia, Middle East, India

Height to 16 in. (40 cm)

Spreads 10 in. (25 cm)

Planting medium 6 in. (15 cm) deep

Full sun

One of the best lavenders; upright, strong bloomer.

Lavandula angustifolia 'Hidcote Superior'. Photograph by Georg Uebelhart, Jelitto Perennial Seeds.

Koeleria glauca

Koeleria macrantha

Linum flavum (Linaceae)

Golden yellow flowers, green
  foliage
Blooms early to late summer
Hardiness zone 5
Accent
Not self sowing
Found in central and southern
  Europe
Height to 8 in. (20 cm)
Spreads 8 in. (20 cm)
Planting medium 10 in. (25 cm)
  deep
Full sun, mixed sun/shade

Nice mass of yellow flowers; requires
irrigation.

Linum perenne (Linaceae)

Light blue flowers, green foliage
Blooms early to late summer
Hardiness zone 5
Accent
Not usually self sowing
Found in western North America
Height to 15 in. (38 cm)
Spreads 8 in. (20 cm)
Planting medium 10 in. (25 cm) deep
Full sun, mixed sun/shade

Pale blue flowers are attractive, but
this plant can be nomadic, as it reseeds sporadically.

Lotus corniculatus

(Papilionaceae)
Yellow flowers, green foliage
Blooms early to late summer
Hardiness zone 5
Groundcover
Not self sowing
Found in Europe, Asia
Height to 4 in. (10 cm)
Spreads 10 in. (25 cm)
Planting medium 6 in. (15 cm) deep
Full sun

Linum flavum. Photograph by Georg Uebelhart, Jelitto Perennial Seeds.

Linum perenne. Photograph by Georg Uebelhart, Jelitto Perennial Seeds.

Grows almost anywhere in the United States. Use to fix nitrogen in the soil. Occasional water required.

Lychnis alpina (Caryophyllaceae)

Dark pink flowers, green foliage
Blooms late spring
Hardiness zone 5
Accent
Not self sowing
Found in northern Europe, Alps, Apennines, Pyrenees
Height to 4 in. (10 cm)
Spreads 6 in. (15 cm)
Planting medium 6 in. (15 cm) deep
Full sun

Nice structure, but not long lived. May need to be replanted or resown to maintain.

Malephora crocea var. *purpureocrocea* 'Tequila Sunrise'

(Aizoaceae)
Orange flowers with yellow centers, blue-green foliage

Blooms midsummer to midautumn
Hardiness zone 8
Groundcover
Not self sowing
Found in South Africa
Height to 10 in. (25 cm)
Spreads 36 in. (91 cm)
Planting medium 4 in. (10 cm) deep
Full sun

Blooms continuously and covers rapidly; salt tolerant.

Lychnis alpina. Photograph by Georg Uebelhart, Jelitto Perennial Seeds.

Lotus corniculatus

Malephora crocea var. *purpureocrocea* 'Tequila Sunrise'

Malephora lutea (Aizoaceae)

Yellow flowers, green foliage
Blooms midsummer to midautumn
Hardiness zone 8
Groundcover
Not self sowing
Found in South Africa
Height to 10 in. (25 cm)
Spreads 36 in. (91 cm)
Planting medium 4 in. (10 cm) deep
Full sun

Not as bold as *M. crocea* var. *purpureocrocea* 'Tequila Sunrise'.

Marrubium incanum (Lamiaceae)

White flowers, silver-green foliage
Blooms early to late summer
Hardiness zone 7
Accent
Not self sowing
Found in Balkans
Height to 16 in. (40 cm)
Spreads 10 in. (25 cm)
Planting medium 6 in. (15 cm) deep
Full sun, mixed sun/shade

Plant serves as larval food for some butterflies. Hairy leaves can appear white. Also use *M. vulgare*.

Nassella tenuissima (Poaceae)

Silver flowers, green foliage
Blooms midsummer
Hardiness zone 8

Marrubium incanum

Malephora lutea

Nassella tenuissima

Accent

Self sowing

Found in western Mediterranean

Height to 15 in. (38 cm)

Spreads 10 in. (25 cm)

Planting medium 6 in. (15 cm) deep

Full sun, mixed sun/shade

Great for structure; stands well after dormancy.

Oenothera caespitosa

(Onagraceae)

White flowers, green foliage

Blooms early to late summer

Hardiness zone 4

Accent

Self sowing

Found in western US

Height to 8 in. (20 cm)

Spreads 12 in. (30 cm)

Planting medium 6 in. (15 cm) deep

Full sun

White, fragrant blooms toward evening. Very drought tolerant once established.

Oenothera macrocarpa (syn. *O. missouriensis*)

(Onagraceae)

Yellow flowers, green foliage

Blooms early to late summer

Hardiness zone 5

Accent

Self sowing

Found in south-central US

Height to 8 in. (20 cm)

Spreads 12 in. (30 cm)

Planting medium 6 in. (15 cm) deep

Full sun

Blooms can be 4 in. (10 cm) wide; attracts night pollinators and moths.

Oenothera caespitosa. Photograph by Georg Uebelhart, Jelitto Perennial Seeds.

Oenothera macrocarpa. Photograph by Georg Uebelhart, Jelitto Perennial Seeds.

Oenothera macrocarpa subsp. *incana* (Onagraceae)
Yellow flowers, silver-gray foliage
Blooms early to late summer
Hardiness zone 4
Accent
Self sowing
Found in south-central US
Height to 8 in. (20 cm)
Spreads 8 in. (20 cm)
Planting medium 6 in. (15 cm) deep
Full sun

Oenothera macrocarpa subsp. *incana*

Foliage adds to plant's ornamental value and drought tolerance.

Opuntia humifusa (syn. *O. compressa*) (Cactaceae)
Yellow flowers, green spines
Blooms early summer
Hardiness zone 4
Accent
Not self sowing
Found in eastern and central US
Height to 8 in. (20 cm)
Spreads 6 in. (15 cm)
Planting medium 4 in. (10 cm) deep
Full sun

Cactus native in the eastern and central United States. Very drought resistant. Sharp spines; avoid planting in public spaces.

Origanum vulgare (Lamiaceae)
Purple flowers, green foliage
Blooms midsummer to midautumn
Hardiness zone 5

Opuntia humifusa. Photograph by Georg Uebelhart, Jelitto Perennial Seeds.

Origanum vulgare

Accent

Not self sowing

Found in Mediterranean to eastern Asia

Height to 14 in. (35 cm)

Spreads 8 in. (20 cm)

Planting medium 6 in. (15 cm) deep

Full sun

Good choice on an herbal green roof; combines the practical and the ornamental.

Orostachys aggregeatum

(Crassulaceae)

White flowers, apple-green foliage

Blooms early autumn to midautumn

Hardiness zone 6

Groundcover

Not self sowing

Found in northern Asia

Height to 6 in. (15 cm)

Spreads 6 in. (15 cm)

Planting medium 4 in. (10 cm) deep

Full sun

Like all *Orostachys*, sends out plantlets on stolons in the spring and summer, creating a mat of green rosettes.

Orostachys boehmeri

(Crassulaceae)

White flowers, gray foliage

Blooms early autumn to midautumn

Hardiness zone 6

Groundcover

Not self sowing

Found in northern Asia

Height to 6 in. (15 cm)

Spreads 6 in. (15 cm)

Planting medium 4 in. (10 cm) deep

Full sun

Unusual gray foliage and dunce cap–shaped flower stalks in the fall.

Orostachys aggregeatum

Orostachys boehmeri

Orostachys fimbriata

(Crassulaceae)

White flowers, gray to brownish red
foliage

Blooms early autumn to midautumn

Hardiness zone 6

Accent

Not self sowing

Found in northern Asia

Height to 6 in. (15 cm)

Spreads 6 in. (15 cm)

Planting medium 4 in. (10 cm) deep

Full sun

Slower growing than *O. boehmeri*.
Amazing foliage color.

Othonna capensis (Asteraceae)

Yellow flowers, blue-green foliage

Blooms late spring to late autumn

Hardiness zone 5

Accent

Not self sowing

Found in South Africa

Height to 3 in. (7 cm)

Spreads 8 in. (20 cm)

Planting medium 4 in. (10 cm) deep

Full sun

Daisylike yellow flowers bloom
continuously in response to bright
sun. May not bloom on cloudy days.
Needs sharp drainage; more likely
to die from winter wet than cold.

Papaver alpinum hybrids

(Papaveraceae)

Mixed color flowers, green foliage

Blooms early summer

Hardiness zone 4

Papaver alpinum. Photograph by Georg
Uebelhart, Jelitto Perennial Seeds.

Orostachys fimbriata

Othonna capensis

Accent

Self sowing

Found in central and southern
  Europe, temperate Asia

Height to 10 in. (25 cm)

Spreads 6 in. (15 cm)

Planting medium 6 in. (15 cm) deep

Full sun, mixed sun/shade

Can be sown directly or from plugs. May act as an annual in hot locations.

Penstemon pinifolius

  (Scrophulariaceae)

Orange-red flowers, green foliage

Blooms early to late summer

Hardiness zone 8

Accent

Not self sowing

Found in southwestern US, Mexico

Height to 8 in. (20 cm)

Spreads 10 in. (25 cm)

Planting medium 6 in. (15 cm) deep

Full sun

Good plant for attracting hummingbirds or for a native green roof in the western US.

Penstemon smallii

  (Scrophulariaceae)

Purple flowers, green foliage

Blooms early to late summer

Accent

Not self sowing

Hardiness zone 6

Found in southeastern US

Height to 22 in. (55 cm)

Spreads 10 in. (25 cm)

Planting medium 6 in. (15 cm) deep

Full sun, mixed sun/shade

Southeastern US native for dry shade. May need irrigation during dry periods.

Penstemon pinifolius. Photograph by Georg Uebelhart, Jelitto Perennial Seeds.

Penstemon smallii. Photograph by Georg Uebelhart, Jelitto Perennial Seeds.

Petrorhagia saxifraga

(Caryophyllaceae)
Light pink flowers, green foliage
Blooms early summer to early
autumn
Hardiness zone 6
Groundcover
Self sowing
Found in southern Europe, Asia
Minor
Height to 7 in. (17 cm)
Spreads 12 in. (30 cm)
Planting medium 6 in. (15 cm) deep
Full sun

Common in Europe. Lots of small pink flowers throughout the summer. May need to be cut back before winter on ornamental roofs.

Phacelia campanularia

(Hydrophyllaceae)
Blue flowers, green foliage
Blooms late spring to early autumn
Hardiness zone 9
Accent
Self sowing
Found in western US
Height to 6 in. (15 cm)
Spreads 8 in. (20 cm)
Planting medium 4 in. (10 cm) deep
Full sun

Stunning blue, bell-shaped flowers appear until weather cools. Best directly sown on the roof.

Phlox subulata (Polemoniaceae)

Pink-lavender flowers, green foliage
Blooms early spring
Hardiness zone 4
Groundcover
Not self sowing
Found in eastern US
Height to 5 in. (12 cm)
Spreads 16 in. (40 cm)
Planting medium 6 in. (15 cm) deep
Full sun, mixed sun/shade

An early season opportunity for color with phlox. *Phlox douglasii* also works well.

Petrorhagia saxifraga

Phacelia campanularia

Poa alpina (Poaceae)

Green flowers, gray-green foliage

Blooms early summer

Hardiness zone 4

Accent

Not self sowing

Found in central Asia, Russia

Height to 4 in. (10 cm)

Spreads 8 in. (20 cm)

Planting medium 6 in. (15 cm) deep

Full sun, mixed sun/shade

Good selection for a high-altitude alpine grass roof. Can be direct sown or planted from plugs. Fertilizing required over time.

Poa chaixii (Poaceae)

Green flowers, green foliage

Blooms early summer

Hardiness zone 5

Accent

Not self sowing

Found in Southwest Asia

Height to 10 in. (25 cm)

Spreads 8 in. (20 cm)

Planting medium 6 in. (15 cm) deep

Full sun, mixed sun/shade

About twice as tall and wider leafed than *P. alpina*, but used in a similar way.

Poa chaixii. Photograph by Georg Uebelhart, Jelitto Perennial Seeds.

Phlox subulata. Photograph by Georg Uebelhart, Jelitto Perennial Seeds.

Poa alpina. Photograph by Georg Uebelhart, Jelitto Perennial Seeds.

Potentilla aurea (Rosaceae)
Yellow flowers, green foliage
Blooms early summer
Hardiness zone 5
Groundcover
Not self sowing
Found in the Carpathians

Height to 6 in. (15 cm)
Spreads 10 in. (25 cm)
Planting medium 6 in. (15 cm) deep
Full sun

Small plant with shiny foliage.

Potentilla crantzii (Rosaceae)
Yellow flowers, green foliage
Blooms midspring
Hardiness zone 5
Groundcover
Not self sowing
Found in northern US, Europe
Height to 6 in. (15 cm)
Spreads 10 in. (25 cm)
Planting medium 6 in. (15 cm) deep
Full sun

Blooms are richer yellow than *P. neumanniana*.

Potentilla neumanniana (syn. *P. verna*) (Rosaceae)
Yellow flowers, green foliage

Potentilla aurea. Photograph by Georg Uebelhart, Jelitto Perennial Seeds.

Potentilla crantzii. Photograph by Georg Uebelhart, Jelitto Perennial Seeds.

Potentilla neumanniana

Blooms midspring to late summer

Hardiness zone 5

Groundcover

Not self sowing

Found in northwestern and central Europe

Height to 9 in. (22 cm)

Spreads 15 in. (38 cm)

Planting medium 6 in. (15 cm) deep

Full sun, mixed sun/shade

Long lasting; may get a little woody. Cut back for more new growth.

Prunella grandiflora

(Lamiaceae)

Purple flowers, green foliage

Blooms midsummer

Hardiness zone 5

Accent

Not self sowing

Found in Europe

Height to 4 in. (10 cm)

Spreads 7 in. (17 cm)

Planting medium 6 in. (15 cm) deep

Full sun, mixed sun/shade

Widely used for European green roofs. Aromatic flowers attract butterflies.

Rosularia chrysantha

(Crassulaceae)

Creamy white flowers, yellow-green foliage

Blooms midsummer

Hardiness zone 6

Accent

Not self sowing

Found in Asia Minor to central Asia

Height to 4 in. (10 cm)

Spreads 5 in. (12 cm)

Planting medium 4 in. (10 cm) deep

Full sun

Small mounds of rosettes provide interest in a border; not fast growing enough to be a groundcover. Foliage turns reddish in winter.

Prunella grandiflora

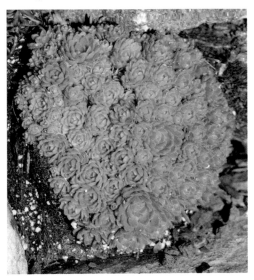

Rosularia chrysantha

Rosularia muratdaghensis

(Crassulaceae)
White flowers, gray-green foliage
Blooms midsummer
Hardiness zone 6
Accent
Not self sowing
Found in Asia Minor to central Asia
Height to 3 in. (7 cm)
Spreads 4 in. (10 cm)
Planting medium 4 in. (10 cm) deep
Full sun

Foliage not as hairy as *R. chrysantha*, but same mounding habit.

Ruschia pulvinaris (Aizoaceae)

Pink flowers, green foliage
Blooms midsummer to midautumn
Accent
Not self sowing
Hardiness zone 8
Found in South Africa
Height to 8 in. (20 cm)
Spreads 8 in. (20 cm)
Planting medium 4 in. (10 cm) deep
Full sun

Good choice for green roofs in western US; dislikes winter wet.

Salvia argentea (Lamiaceae)

White flowers, silver-gray foliage
Blooms midsummer to late summer

Salvia argentea

Rosularia muratdaghensis

Ruschia pulvinaris

Hardiness zone 5

Accent

Not self sowing

Found in southern Europe, North Africa

Height to 25 in. (63 cm)

Spreads 12 in. (30 cm)

Planting medium 6 in. (15 cm) deep

Full sun

Large, fuzzy leaves are dramatic. Remove flower stalks before the seed ripens to prolong its life.

Salvia jurisicii (Lamiaceae)

Pink-lilac flowers, green foliage

Blooms midsummer to late summer

Hardiness zone 6

Accent

Not self sowing

Found in the Balkans

Height to 10 in. (25 cm)

Spreads 12 in. (30 cm)

Planting medium 6 in. (15 cm) deep

Full sun

Good choice for Mediterranean conditions; fine-textured foliage.

Salvia officinalis (Lamiaceae)

Lilac flowers, gray-green foliage

Blooms early to late summer

Hardiness zone 5

Accent

Not self sowing

Found in the Mediterranean

Height to 20 in. (50 cm)

Spreads 12 in. (30 cm)

Planting medium 6 in. (15 cm) deep

Full sun

Used for culinary or ornamental green roof. Can get woody over time; cut back to keep the growth fresh.

Salvia jurisicii. Photograph by Georg Uebelhart, Jelitto Perennial Seeds.

Salvia officinalis

Salvia pratensis (Lamiaceae)

Blue flowers, green foliage
Blooms early to late summer
Hardiness zone 3
Accent
Not self sowing
Found in Europe
Height to 23 in. (58 cm)
Spreads 12 in. (30 cm)
Planting medium 6 in. (15 cm) deep
Full sun

Long-lived plant stays upright. Will not tolerate extended periods with wet medium.

Santolina rosmarinifolia

(Asteraceae)
Yellow flowers, blue-green foliage
Blooms late summer
Hardiness zone 7
Accent
Not self sowing
Found in southeastern Spain
Height to 12 in. (30 cm)
Spreads 12 in. (30 cm)
Planting medium 6 in. (15 cm) deep
Full sun

Yellow flowers sit nicely above the upright foliage.

Saponaria ocymoides

(Caryophyllaceae)
Pink flowers, green foliage
Blooms early to late summer
Hardiness zone 4
Groundcover
Not self sowing
Found in mountains of southern Europe
Height to 12 in. (30 cm)
Spreads 12 in. (30 cm)
Planting medium 6 in. (15 cm) deep
Full sun

Salvia pratensis

Santolina rosmarinifolia. Photograph by Georg Uebelhart, Jelitto Perennial Seeds.

Low groundcover is long lived; needs irrigation.

Scabiosa columbaria 'Misty Butterflies' (Dipsacaceae)

Pink-purple flowers, green foliage

Blooms early summer to early autumn

Hardiness zone 6

Accent

Not self sowing

Found in Europe, Africa, Asia

Height to 10 in. (25 cm)

Spreads 10 in. (25 cm)

Planting medium 6 in. (15 cm) deep

Full sun, mixed sun/shade

Colorful; another good choice is *S. columbaria* 'Pincushion Pink'.

Scilla mischtschenkoana (syn. S. tubergeniana) (Hyacinthaceae)

Light blue flowers, green foliage

Blooms late winter, early spring

Hardiness zone 3

Accent

Not self sowing

Found in Iran, Russia

Height to 5 in. (12 cm)

Spreads 6 in. (15 cm)

Planting medium 6 in. (15 cm) deep

Full sun, mixed sun/shade

Early blooming plant is very cold hardy. Bulbs need water during a dry spring.

Scabiosa columbaria 'Misty Butterflies'. Photograph by Georg Uebelhart, Jelitto Perennial Seeds.

Saponaria ocymoides. Photograph by Georg Uebelhart, Jelitto Perennial Seeds.

Scilla mischtschenkoana. Photograph by Georg Uebelhart, Jelitto Perennial Seeds.

Scutellaria alpina (Lamiaceae)

Purple flowers with white lips, green foliage
Blooms early to late summer
Hardiness zone 5
Accent
Not self sowing
Found in mountains of southern Europe to Siberia
Height to 10 in. (25 cm)
Spreads 8 in. (20 cm)
Planting medium 6 in. (15 cm) deep
Full sun, mixed sun/shade

Takes heat well; flowers sometimes blue and white. Needs irrigation.

Scutellaria alpina 'Moonbeam'

(Lamiaceae)
Pale yellow flowers, green foliage
Blooms late spring to late summer
Hardiness zone 5
Accent
Not self sowing
Found in mountains of southern Europe to Siberia
Height to 10 in. (25 cm)
Spreads 8 in. (20 cm)
Planting medium 6 in. (15 cm) deep
Full sun, mixed sun/shade

Buttery yellow flowers have a golden lip; long bloom period.

Sedum acre 'Aureum'

(Crassulaceae)
Yellow flowers, green foliage
Blooms early to late summer
Hardiness zone 4
Groundcover
Not self sowing
Found in Europe, western and northern Asia
Height to 2 in. (5 cm)
Spreads 8 in. (20 cm)
Planting medium 4 in. (10 cm) deep
Full sun

Early growth has gold tips on the new leaves. Dies back in hot, humid summers.

Scutellaria alpina. Photograph by Georg Uebelhart, Jelitto Perennial Seeds.

Scutellaria alpina 'Moonbeam'. Photograph by Georg Uebelhart, Jelitto Perennial Seeds.

Sedum acre 'Oktoberfest'

(Crassulaceae)
White flowers, green foliage
Blooms early to late summer
Hardiness zone 4
Groundcover
Not self sowing
Found in Europe, western and
  northern Asia
Height to 2 in. (5 cm)
Spreads 8 in. (20 cm)
Planting medium 4 in. (10 cm)
  deep
Full sun

White flowers en masse resemble beer foam. Introduced by Jelitto Perennial Seeds.

Sedum aizoon 'Euphorbioides'

(Crassulaceae)
Yellow flowers, green foliage
Blooms midsummer
Accent
Not self sowing
Hardiness zone 4

Found in Europe, western and
  northern Asia
Height to 10 in. (25 cm)
Spreads 8 in. (20 cm)
Planting medium 4 in. (10 cm) deep
Full sun

Shrubby plant with red stems and strong foliage.

Sedum acre 'Oktoberfest'

Sedum acre 'Aureum'

Sedum aizoon 'Euphorbioides'

Sedum album (Crassulaceae)

White flowers, green foliage
Blooms midsummer
Hardiness zone 4
Groundcover
Not self sowing
Found in Europe, western and
  northern Asia
Height to 6 in. (15 cm)
Spreads 8 in. (20 cm)
Planting medium 4 in. (10 cm) deep
Full sun

A staple for green roofs. Viable from seeds, cuttings, and plugs. Foliage turns red in winter.

Sedum album 'Chloroticum'

(Crassulaceae)
White flowers, green foliage
Blooms midsummer
Hardiness zone 4
Groundcover
Not self sowing
Found in Europe, western and
  northern Asia
Height to 2 in. (5 cm)
Spreads 6 in. (15 cm)
Planting medium 4 in. (10 cm) deep
Full sun

A true evergreen with very small leaves. Slow growing and not a reliable flowerer.

Sedum album 'Coral Carpet'

(Crassulaceae)
White flowers, green and red
  foliage
Blooms midsummer
Hardiness zone 4
Groundcover
Self sowing
Found in Europe, western and
  northern Asia
Height to 2 in. (5 cm)
Spreads 8 in. (20 cm)
Planting medium 4 in. (10 cm) deep
Full sun

Very dense and low-growing cultivar of *S. album*; foliage turns red in

Sedum album

Sedum album 'Chloroticum'

drought, stress, and cold. Not a reliable flowerer.

Sedum album 'France'

(Crassulaceae)

White flowers, green foliage with red highlights

Blooms midsummer

Hardiness zone 4

Groundcover

Not self sowing

Found in Europe, western and northern Asia

Height to 8 in. (20 cm)

Spreads 8 in. (20 cm)

Planting medium 4 in. (10 cm) deep

Full sun

Large-leaf form used for more presence and structure.

Sedum album subsp. tereti-folium 'Murale' (Crassulaceae)

White flowers, green and red foliage

Blooms midsummer

Hardiness zone 4

Groundcover

Not self sowing

Found in Europe, western and northern Asia

Height to 6 in. (15 cm)

Spreads 8 in. (20 cm)

Planting medium 4 in. (10 cm) deep

Full sun

Red foliage color throughout much of the year. Often sold mistakenly as *S.* 'Coral Carpet'.

Sedum album subsp. *teretifolium* 'Murale'

Sedum album 'Coral Carpet'

Sedum album 'France'

Sedum apoleipon

(Crassulaceae)
White flowers, blue-green foliage
Blooms midsummer
Hardiness zone 7
Accent
Not self sowing
Found in north-facing mountains of
  central Greece
Height to 3 in. (7 cm)
Spreads 8 in. (20 cm)
Planting medium 4 in. (10 cm)
  deep
Full sun

Slow growing, mounding plant good in tight areas.

Sedum cauticola 'Bertram Anderson' (Crassulaceae)

Pink flowers, purple-black foliage
Blooms early autumn
Hardiness zone 4
Accent
Not self sowing
Found in Japan
Height to 8 in. (20 cm)
Spreads 8 in. (20 cm)
Planting medium 4 in. (10 cm) deep
Full sun

Almost black foliage in the summer sun. Slow growing; needs some care for establishment.

Sedum cauticola 'Lidakense'

(Crassulaceae)
Pink flowers, blue-gray foliage
Blooms early autumn
Hardiness zone 4
Accent
Not self sowing
Found in Japan
Height to 8 in. (20 cm)
Spreads 8 in. (20 cm)
Planting medium 4 in. (10 cm) deep
Full sun

Can be used in drifts.

Sedum apoleipon

Sedum cauticola 'Bertram Anderson'

Sedum dasyphyllum

(Crassulaceae)

White flowers, blue-green foliage

Blooms midsummer

Hardiness zone 8

Accent

Not self sowing

Found in central Europe to Mediterranean coastline

Height to 3 in. (7 cm)

Spreads 8 in. (20 cm)

Planting medium 4 in. (10 cm) deep

Full sun

Tiny leaves root easily and will pop up around the roof. More an accent plant than a reliable groundcover.

Sedum diffusum (Crassulaceae)

White flowers, blue-green foliage

Blooms midsummer

Hardiness zone 8

Groundcover

Not self sowing

Found in northeastern Mexico

Height to 6 in. (15 cm)

Spreads 8 in. (20 cm)

Planting medium 4 in. (10 cm) deep

Full sun

Very fast grower; performed well at the North Carolina State plant trials.

Sedum cauticola 'Lidakense'

Sedum dasyphyllum

Sedum diffusum

Sedum divergens (Crassulaceae)
Yellow flowers, pink and green foliage

Blooms midsummer

Hardiness zone 4

Accent

Not self sowing

Found in Pacific coastal areas of US

Height to 4 in. (10 cm)

Spreads 8 in. (20 cm)

Planting medium 4 in. (10 cm) deep

Full sun

Native to western US. Does not like hot, humid summers in the eastern and midwestern US.

Sedum ewersii (Crassulaceae)
Pink flowers, blue-green foliage

Blooms midsummer

Hardiness zone 4

Accent

Not self sowing

Found in western Himalayas to Mongolia

Height to 4 in. (10 cm)

Spreads 8 in. (20 cm)

Planting medium 4 in. (10 cm) deep

Full sun

Good slow-growing plant; needs more care than the toughest of sedums, but much less than most other plants.

Sedum forsterianum subsp. *elegans* (Crassulaceae)
Yellow flowers, red-green and blue-green foliage

Blooms midsummer

Hardiness zone 5

Accent

Not self sowing

Found in Europe, Asia Minor

Height to 8 in. (20 cm)

Spreads 8 in. (20 cm)

Planting medium 4 in. (10 cm) deep

Full sun

Best used where summer heat and humidity are low.

Sedum divergens

Sedum ewersii

Sedum 'Green Spruce'

(Crassulaceae)
Yellow flowers, green foliage
Blooms early to late summer
Hardiness zone 4
Accent
Not self sowing
Found in Europe, western and
   northern Asia
Height to 6 in. (15 cm)
Spreads 8 in. (20 cm)
Planting medium 4 in. (10 cm)
   deep
Full sun

Looks like a tiny Douglas-fir, with umbrella-like yellow flowers. Slow to fill in.

Sedum griseum (Crassulaceae)

Yellow flowers, blue-green foliage
Blooms late spring
Hardiness zone 10
Accent
Not self sowing
Found in Mexico
Height to 8 in. (20 cm)
Spreads 8 in. (20 cm)
Planting medium 4 in. (10 cm)
   deep
Full sun

Substitute for *S. rupestre* (syn. *S. relexum*) in regions without frost. Will need occasional water in periods of drought.

Sedum 'Green Spruce'

Sedum forsterianum subsp. *elegans*

Sedum griseum

Sedum hispanicum (Crassulaceae)
  White flowers, blue-green foliage
  Blooms midsummer
  Hardiness zone 6
  Groundcover
  Not self sowing
  Found from Sicily to Turkey

Height to 3 in. (7 cm)
Spreads 8 in. (20 cm)
Planting medium 4 in. (10 cm) deep
Full sun

Rapid growing low sedum. Emits blues, pinks, and purples from the foliage, depending on temperature, water, and nutrients.

Sedum hispanicum

Sedum hybridum 'Czar's Gold'
  (Crassulaceae)
  Yellow flowers, green foliage
  Blooms late spring
  Hardiness zone 4
  Groundcover
  Not self sowing
  Found in Siberia and Mongolia
  Height to 6 in. (15 cm)
  Spreads 8 in. (20 cm)
  Planting medium 4 in. (10 cm) deep
  Full sun

Good color for winter interest. Reliable from seed.

Sedum hybridum 'Immergrünchen' (Crassulaceae)
  Yellow flowers, red and green foliage
  Blooms midsummer to late summer
  Hardiness zone 4
  Groundcover
  Not self sowing
  Found in Siberia and Mongolia
  Height to 6 in. (15 cm)
  Spreads 8 in. (20 cm)
  Planting medium 4 in. (10 cm) deep
  Full sun

Keeps its foliage through much of

Sedum hybridum 'Czar's Gold'

the winter. Similar in look to *S. kamtschaticum* but slower growing.

Sedum kamtschaticum

(Crassulaceae)
Yellow flowers, green foliage
Blooms midsummer
Hardiness zone 4
Groundcover
Not self sowing
Found in Ural Mountains to
  Mongolia
Height to 6 in. (15 cm)
Spreads 8 in. (20 cm)
Planting medium 4 in. (10 cm) deep
Full sun

From a distance looks similar to pachysandra. Survived more than 80 days without water in Michigan State trials.

Sedum kamtschaticum var. floriferum 'Weihenstephaner Gold' (Crassulaceae)

Yellow flowers, green foliage
Blooms midsummer
Hardiness zone 4
Groundcover
Not self sowing
Found in northeastern China
Height to 4 in. (10 cm)
Spreads 12 in. (30 cm)
Planting medium 4 in. (10 cm) deep
Full sun

Very floriferous. Red rosettes in the winter; strong green foliage in the summer.

Sedum hybridum 'Immergrünchen'

Sedum kamtschaticum

Sedum kamtschaticum var. floriferum 'Weihenstephaner Gold'

Sedum kamtschaticum var. kamtschaticum 'Variegatum'

(Crassulaceae)
Yellow flowers, green foliage with white variegation
Blooms midsummer
Hardiness zone 4
Groundcover
Not self sowing
Found in Ural Mountains to Mongolia
Height to 6 in. (15 cm)
Spreads 8 in. (20 cm)
Planting medium 4 in. (10 cm) deep
Full sun

Creamy variegation gives plant a reflective quality. As tough as its green counterpart, *S. kamtschaticum*.

Sedum lanceolatum

(Crassulaceae)
Yellow flowers, green foliage
Blooms midsummer
Hardiness zone 6
Accent
Not usually self sowing
Found in western US and Canada
Height to 4 in. (10 cm)
Spreads 6 in. (15 cm)
Planting medium 4 in. (10 cm) deep
Full sun

Rocky Mountain native. Will self sow in a limited area only.

Sedum lineare 'Variegatum'

(Crassulaceae)
Yellow flowers, green foliage with white or pink edges
Blooms midsummer
Hardiness zone 7
Groundcover
Not self sowing
Found in Japan
Height to 6 in. (15 cm)
Spreads 8 in. (20 cm)
Planting medium 4 in. (10 cm) deep
Full sun

Used to hang over the edges of a roof or as a drip edge. Much better

Sedum kamtschaticum var. *kamtschaticum* 'Variegatum'

Sedum lanceolatum

behaved than *S. sarmentosum*, but not as hardy.

Sedum lydium

(Crassulaceae)
Yellow flowers, green to red foliage
Blooms midsummer
Hardiness zone 8
Accent
Not self sowing
Found in Turkey
Height to 4 in. (10 cm)
Spreads 6 in. (15 cm)
Planting medium 4 in. (10 cm) deep
Full sun

Tolerates wet conditions. Good winter color from dark green to red.

Sedum makinoi

(Crassulaceae)
Yellow flowers, green foliage
Blooms midsummer
Hardiness zone 7
Groundcover
Not self sowing
Found in Japan
Height to 4 in. (10 cm)
Spreads 8 in. (20 cm)
Planting medium 4 in. (10 cm)
  deep
Full sun, mixed sun/shade

Several strong varieties and/or cultivars range from yellow to lime green foliage. Needs some shade.

Sedum makinoi

Sedum lineare 'Variegatum'

Sedum lydium

Sedum 'Matrona'

(Crassulaceae)
Pink flowers, green-gray foliage
Blooms early autumn
Hardiness zone 6
Accent
Not self sowing
Found in Japan
Height to 12 in. (30 cm)
Spreads 10 in. (25 cm)
Planting medium 4 in. (10 cm) deep
Full sun

Sedum 'Matrona'

Sedum mexicanum

Provides some height when planted in thin medium.

Sedum mexicanum

(Crassulaceae)
Yellow flowers, green foliage
Blooms early summer
Hardiness zone 8
Groundcover
Not self sowing
Found in East Asia and Central America
Height to 4 in. (10 cm)
Spreads 15 in. (38 cm)
Planting medium 4 in. (10 cm) deep
Full sun/mixed sun/shade

Rapid spreader; not a reliable bloomer.

Sedum middendorffianum var. diffusum (Crassulaceae)

Yellow flowers, green foliage
Blooms midsummer
Hardiness zone 5
Groundcover
Not self sowing
Found in Siberia, China, Japan
Height to 4 in. (10 cm)
Spreads 8 in. (20 cm)
Planting medium 4 in. (10 cm) deep
Full sun

A star from the Michigan State plant trials. Very durable, with a carpet of yellow flowers. Foliage turns russet in winter.

Sedum moranense (Crassulaceae)

White flowers, green foliage

Blooms midsummer

Hardiness zone 8

Groundcover

Not self sowing

Found in Mexico

Height to 3 in. (7 cm)

Spreads 12 in. (30 cm)

Planting medium 4 in. (10 cm) deep

Full sun

Very dense growth; excellent option for California and the southern US. Foliage has pink or red tinges in winter.

Sedum ochroleucum

(Crassulaceae)

Pale yellow flowers, blue-green foliage with pink tinges

Blooms midsummer

Hardiness zone 5

Accent

Not self sowing

Found in southern Europe

Height to 8 in. (20 cm)

Spreads 8 in. (20 cm)

Planting medium 4 in. (10 cm) deep

Full sun

Similar to *S. rupestre* (syn. *S. reflexum*), but with a straw-colored flower and pink highlights on the foliage as the weather cools.

Sedum moranense

Sedum middendorffianum var. *diffusum*

Sedum ochroleucum

Sedum oreganum (Crassulaceae)
Yellow flowers, green foliage
Blooms midsummer to late summer
Hardiness zone 5
Accent
Not self sowing
Found on Pacific Coast
Height to 4 in. (10 cm)
Spreads 8 in. (20 cm)
Planting medium 4 in. (10 cm) deep
Full sun, mixed sun/shade

Staple plant for the Pacific Northwest; in the eastern US may need some shade and irrigation.

Sedum pachyclados
(Crassulaceae)
White flowers, blue-green foliage
Blooms early summer to midsummer
Hardiness zone 5
Groundcover
Not self sowing
Found in Pakistan, Afghanistan
Height to 3 in. (7 cm)
Spreads 6 in. (15 cm)
Planting medium 4 in. (10 cm) deep
Full sun, mixed sun/shade

Good choice for wet and shade. Slow grower can take altitude.

Sedum pluricaule 'Rosen-teppich' (Crassulaceae)
Pink flowers, blue-green foliage
Blooms late spring to late summer
Hardiness zone 4
Groundcover
Not self sowing
Found in eastern Siberia
Height to 3 in. (7 cm)
Spreads 6 in. (15 cm)
Planting medium 4 in. (10 cm) deep
Full sun

Tight groundcover when established. May take some care to

Sedum oreganum. Photograph by Georg Uebelhart, Jelitto Perennial Seeds.

Sedum pachyclados

establish if planting in the summer. Foliage has pink tinges in cold weather.

Sedum pluricaule var. *ezawe*
(Crassulaceae)
Pink flowers, green to purple foliage
Blooms midsummer to late summer
Hardiness zone 6
Groundcover
Not self sowing
Found in eastern Siberia
Height to 3 in. (7 cm)
Spreads 6 in. (15 cm)
Planting medium 4 in. (10 cm) deep
Full sun

Attractive tightly clustered leaves in shades of purple. Foliage becomes more colorful in response to sun and drought; use for foliage more than flower.

Sedum pulchellum (Crassulaceae)
Pale pink flowers, green foliage
Blooms late spring
Hardiness zone 8
Groundcover
Self sowing
Found in eastern Alps
Height to 4 in. (10 cm)
Spreads 8 in. (20 cm)
Planting medium 4 in. (10 cm) deep
Full sun

Best planted from seed directly sown on the roof. Great early pink bloom.

Sedum pluricaule 'Rosenteppich'

Sedum pluricaule var. *ezawe*

Sedum pulchellum. Photograph by Georg Uebelhart, Jelitto Perennial Seeds.

Sedum ×rubrotinctum

(Crassulaceae)
Yellow flowers, green to red foliage
Blooms midsummer
Hardiness zone 10
Accent
Not self sowing
Found in Latin America
Height to 8 in. (20 cm)
Spreads 6 in. (15 cm)
Planting medium 4 in. (10 cm) deep
Full sun

Shiny, succulent leaves turn bright red in sunlight. Highly ornamental.

Sedum ×rubrotinctum (dwarf form) (Crassulaceae)

Yellow flowers, green to red foliage
Blooms midsummer
Hardiness zone 10
Accent
Not self sowing
Found in Latin America
Height to 4 in. (10 cm)
Spreads 4 in. (10 cm)
Planting medium 4 in. (10 cm) deep
Full sun

Good selection for small areas. Best used where it can be viewed up close.

Sedum rupestre (syn. *S. reflexum*) (Crassulaceae)

Yellow flowers, blue-green foliage
Blooms midsummer
Hardiness zone 4

Sedum rupestre

Sedum ×rubrotinctum

Sedum ×rubrotinctum (dwarf form)

Accent
Not self sowing
Found in central and western
  Europe
Height to 8 in. (20 cm)
Spreads 8 in. (20 cm)
Planting medium 4 in. (10 cm) deep
Full sun

Widely used on green roofs in northern US. Strong blue-green foliage color and tall, striking yellow blooms. May fade in wet summers, but reappears in dry periods.

Sedum rupestre 'Angelina'

  (Crassulaceae)
Yellow flowers, green to yellow
  foliage
Blooms midsummer
Hardiness zone 4
Accent
Not self sowing
Found in central and western
  Europe

Height to 5 in. (12 cm)
Spreads 8 in. (20 cm)
Planting medium 4 in. (10 cm) deep
Full sun

Does not reliably flower; winter interest.

Sedum sarmentosum

  (Crassulaceae)
Yellow flowers, light green foliage
Blooms midsummer to late
  summer
Hardiness zone 5
Groundcover
Not self sowing
Found in Asia
Height to 3 in. (7 cm)
Spreads 36 in. (91 cm)
Planting medium 4 in. (10 cm) deep
Full sun

Keep an eye on this one—can be aggressive and overrun other plants. Useful as a hanging plant.

Sedum rupestre 'Angelina'

Sedum sarmentosum

Sedum sediforme (Crassulaceae)
Yellow flowers, blue-green foliage
Blooms midsummer
Hardiness zone 7
Accent
Not self sowing
Found in southern Europe, North
  Africa
Height to 10 in. (25 cm)
Spreads 8 in. (20 cm)
Planting medium 4 in. (10 cm) deep
Full sun

Good blue alternative to *S. rupestre*, with thicker leaves and stronger presence.

Sedum sediforme

Sedum selskianum

Sedum selskianum (Crassulaceae)
Yellow flowers, green foliage
Blooms midsummer
Hardiness zone 4
Accent
Not self sowing
Found in northern China and
  southern Mongolia, Kazakhstan,
  and Russia
Height to 8 in. (20 cm)
Spreads 8 in. (20 cm)
Planting medium 4 in. (10 cm) deep
Full sun

Often mislabeled in the trade. All parts of the plant are hairy. Mounds of green foliage in late summer.

Sedum sexangulare
(Crassulaceae)
Yellow flowers, green foliage
Blooms midsummer
Hardiness zone 4
Groundcover
Not self sowing
Found in central Europe
Height to 4 in. (10 cm)
Spreads 8 in. (20 cm)
Planting medium 4 in. (10 cm) deep
Full sun, mixed sun/shade, shade

A highly adaptable foundation plant for any location. Can thrive in shade and moisture. Foliage turns russet color in cool weather.

Sedum sichotense (Crassulaceae)
Yellow flowers, green foliage
Blooms midsummer
Hardiness zone 4
Accent

Not self sowing
Found in eastern Ukraine
Height to 6 in. (15 cm)
Spreads 8 in. (20 cm)
Planting medium 4 in. (10 cm) deep
Full sun

Great burgundy red fall and winter color reminiscent of maple leaves. More clump forming by nature.

Sedum sieboldii (Crassulaceae)
Pink flowers, blue-green foliage
with pink tinges

Blooms midautumn
Hardiness zone 6
Accent
Not self sowing
Found in Japan
Height to 8 in. (20 cm)
Spreads 8 in. (20 cm)
Planting medium 4 in. (10 cm) deep
Full sun

Mounding habit. Needs more care to establish than groundcover sedums.

Sedum sexangulare

Sedum sichotense

Sedum sieboldii

Sedum spathulifolium

(Crassulaceae)
Yellow flowers, gray foliage
Blooms midsummer to late summer
Hardiness zone 6
Groundcover
Not self sowing
Found in US Northwest
Height to 4 in. (10 cm)
Spreads 6 in. (15 cm)
Planting medium 4 in. (10 cm) deep
Full sun, mixed sun/shade

Sedum spathulifolium. Photograph by Georg Uebelhart, Jelitto Perennial Seeds.

Loves the moist Pacific Northwest, but does not do well in the midwestern or eastern US.

Sedum spurium 'Fuldaglut'

(Crassulaceae)
Pink flowers, green to red foliage
Blooms midsummer to late summer
Hardiness zone 5
Groundcover
Not self sowing
Found in Caucasus range to
   Armenia and northern Iran
Height to 6 in. (15 cm)
Spreads 8 in. (20 cm)
Planting medium 4 in. (10 cm) deep
Full sun, mixed sun/shade

A standard for red foliage in fall and winter; very tough plant does well in some shade, but foliage won't be as red.

Sedum spurium 'John Creech'

(Crassulaceae)
Pink flowers, green foliage
Blooms midsummer to late summer
Hardiness zone 5

Sedum spurium 'Fuldaglut'

Sedum spurium 'John Creech'

Groundcover

Not self sowing

Found in Caucasus range to
   Armenia and northern Iran

Height to 6 in. (15 cm)

Spreads 8 in. (20 cm)

Planting medium 4 in. (10 cm) deep

Full sun

Has the widest geographic range of the *spurium* sedums; used in US from New England to Georgia.

Sedum spurium 'Roseum'

(Crassulaceae)

Pink flowers, green foliage

Blooms autumn

Hardiness zone 4

Groundcover

Not self sowing

Found in Caucasus range to
   Armenia and northern Iran

Height to 6 in. (15 cm)

Spreads 8 in. (20 cm)

Planting medium 4 in. (10 cm) deep

Full sun

Has proven tough in drought and is a good candidate for cuttings planted directly on the roof.

Sedum spurium 'Summer Glory' (Crassulaceae)

Dark pink flowers, green foliage

Blooms midsummer to late summer

Hardiness zone 5

Groundcover

Not self sowing

Found in Caucasus range to
   Armenia and northern Iran

Height to 6 in. (15 cm)

Spreads 8 in. (20 cm)

Planting medium 4 in. (10 cm) deep

Full sun

Good selection for its flower and foliage colors.

Sedum spurium 'Roseum'

Sedum spurium 'Summer Glory'

Sedum spurium var. album

(Crassulaceae)
White flowers, green foliage
Blooms autumn
Hardiness zone 4
Groundcover
Not self sowing
Found in Caucasus range to
  Armenia and northern Iran
Height to 6 in. (15 cm)
Spreads 8 in. (20 cm)
Planting medium 4 in. (10 cm) deep
Full sun, mixed sun/shade, shade

Late-season white flower. *Sedum spurium* 'Album Superbum' is a similar choice.

Sedum spurium 'Voodoo'

(Crassulaceae)
Blood red flowers, red foliage
Blooms autumn
Hardiness zone 4
Groundcover
Not self sowing
Found in Caucasus range to
  Armenia and northern Iran
Height to 6 in. (15 cm)
Spreads 8 in. (20 cm)
Planting medium 4 in. (10 cm) deep
Full sun

Dark red foliage into winter. Attractive in drifts.

Sedum stahlii

(Crassulaceae)
Yellow flowers, green to pink foliage
Blooms summer
Hardiness zone 8
Accent
Not self sowing
Found in Mexican states of Puebla
  and Veracruz, Pacific to Carib-
  bean coasts of southern Mexico
Height to 6 in. (15 cm)
Spreads 6 in. (15 cm)
Planting medium 4 in. (10 cm) deep
Full sun

Sedum spurium var. *album*

Sedum spurium 'Voodoo'. Photograph by Georg Uebelhart, Jelitto Perennial Seeds.

Good choice for roofs in southern US. Interesting form with leaves that drop and root.

Sedum stefco

(Crassulaceae)
White flowers, green to red foliage
Blooms late summer/early fall
Hardiness zone 5
Groundcover
Not self sowing
Found in southwestern Bulgaria

Sedum stahlii

Height to 2 in. (5 cm)
Spreads 8 in. (20 cm)
Planting medium 4 in. (10 cm) deep
Full sun

Tight, low growth. Vivid winter red foliage. Very tough; can be used in high wind areas.

Sedum stenopetalum

(Crassulaceae)
Yellow flower, green foliage
Blooms summer
Hardiness zone 5
Accent
Self sowing
Found in western North America
Height to 5 in. (12 cm)
Spreads 6 in. (15 cm)
Planting medium 4 in. (10 cm) deep
Full sun

Good native of western US. Foliage turns red in winter.

Sedum stefco

Sedum stenopetalum

Sedum stoloniferum

(Crassulaceae)
Pink flowers, light green foliage
Blooms midsummer
Hardiness zone 7
Groundcover
Not self sowing
Found in Eastern Cordillera of the
   Andes
Height to 8 in. (20 cm)
Spreads 10 in. (25 cm)
Planting medium 4 in. (10 cm) deep
Mixed sun/shade, shade

Good choice for dry shade; covers
well. Foliage reflects soft light.

Sedum telephioides

(Crassulaceae)
White flowers, blue-green foliage
Blooms early autumn
Hardiness zone 5
Accent
Not self sowing
Found in Pennsylvania
Height to 24 in. (60 cm)
Spreads 10 in. (25 cm)
Planting medium 4 in. (10 cm) deep
Full sun

The only tall native sedum suitable
for green roof application. Pink
stems may be floppy in rich
medium.

Sedum telephium 'Emperor's Waves' (Crassulaceae)

Purple-red flowers, blue-green
   foliage
Blooms late summer
Hardiness zone 6
Accent
Not self sowing
Found in Japan
Height to 16 in. (40 cm)
Spreads 8 in. (20 cm)
Planting medium 4 in. (10 cm) deep
Full sun

Sedum stoloniferum

Sedum telephioides

Exciting dark foliage. Good for contrast in both height and color.

Sedum ternatum (Crassulaceae)
White flowers, green foliage
Blooms midsummer
Hardiness zone 5
Groundcover
Not self sowing
Found in eastern US
Height to 3 in. (7 cm)
Spreads 8 in. (20 cm)
Planting medium 4 in. (10 cm) deep
Mixed sun/shade, shade

Native of eastern US found along stream edges. Drought tolerant, but needs protection from full sun. Use in shadows or near drains.

Sedum tetractinum (Crassulaceae)
Yellow flowers with green to bronze foliage
Blooms spring

Hardiness zone 7
Groundcover
Not self sowing
Found in Hunan-Kwangtung border, China
Height to 4 in. (10 cm)
Spreads 10 in. (25 cm)
Planting medium 4 in. (10 cm) deep
Full sun

A favorite of plantsman Bobby Saul, this is a rapid grower with nice bronze fall foliage.

Sedum ternatum

Sedum telephium 'Emperor's Waves'.
Photograph by Georg Uebelhart, Jelitto Perennial Seeds.

Sedum tetractinum

Sedum urvillei (Crassulaceae)
Yellow flowers, blue-green foliage
Blooms late summer
Hardiness zone 6
Groundcover
Not self sowing
Found in eastern Europe, Middle
    East
Height to 2 in. (5 cm)
Spreads 6 in. (15 cm)
Planting medium 4 in. (10 cm) deep
Full sun

Tight growth habit, able to take the summer heat. Foliage turns red in winter.

Sempervivum arachnoideum 'Sparkle' (Crassulaceae)
Pink flowers, yellow-green to red
    foliage
Blooms summer
Hardiness zone 5
Accent
Not self sowing
Found in Alps, Asia Minor, Caucasus
    mountains, to Iran
Height to 5 in. (12 cm)
Spreads 6 in. (15 cm)
Planting medium 4 in. (10 cm) deep
Full sun

Spider web–like hairy foliage adds interest. A large selection of *S. arachnoideum* varieties/cultivars are suitable for green roofs.

Sempervivum 'Blue Boy' (Crassulaceae)
Pink flowers, blue-green foliage
Blooms summer
Hardiness zone 5
Accent
Not self sowing
Found in Alps, Asia Minor, Cauca-
    sus mountains, to Iran
Height to 6 in. (15 cm)
Spreads 6 in. (15 cm)
Planting medium 4 in. (10 cm) deep
Full sun

Large rosettes; will mound over time. Hundreds of *Sempervivum* varieties and cultivars exist in the

Sedum urvillei

Sempervivum arachnoideum 'Sparkle'

trade and work as well; mentioned here are representative examples.

Sempervivum 'Georgette'

(Crassulaceae)
Pink flowers, green to red foliage
Blooms summer
Hardiness zone 5
Accent
Not self sowing
Found in Alps, Asia Minor, Caucasus
mountains, to Iran
Height to 6 in. (15 cm)
Spreads 6 in. (15 cm)
Planting medium 4 in. (10 cm) deep
Full sun

Bright red foliage in winter. Tough in drought; mounding habit.

Sempervivum 'Oddity'

(Crassulaceae)
Pink flowers, bright green foliage
Blooms summer
Hardiness zone 5
Accent
Not self sowing
Found in Alps, Asia Minor, Caucasus
mountains, to Iran
Height to 6 in. (15 cm)
Spreads 6 in. (15 cm)
Planting medium 4 in. (10 cm) deep
Full sun

Unusual looking plant, with pincushion of tubelike leaves.

Sempervivum 'Oddity'

Sempervivum 'Blue Boy'

Sempervivum 'Georgette'

Sempervivum 'Saturn'

(Crassulaceae)
Pink flowers, reddish green foliage
Blooms summer
Hardiness zone 5
Accent
Not self sowing
Found in Alps, Asia Minor,
   Caucasus mountains, to Iran
Height to 6 in. (15 cm)
Spreads 6 in. (15 cm)
Planting medium 4 in. (10 cm) deep
Full sun

Medium size rosettes with highlights of pink in cooler weather.

Sempervivum 'Silver Thaw'

(Crassulaceae)
Pink flowers, silver-green foliage
Blooms summer
Hardiness zone 5
Accent
Not self sowing
Found in Alps, Asia Minor,
   Caucasus mountains, to Iran
Height to 4 in. (10 cm)
Spreads 6 in. (15 cm)
Planting medium 4 in. (10 cm) deep
Full sun

Small, tight rosettes; easily forms dense mounds.

Sesleria autumnalis

(Poaceae)
Golden brown flowers, green to
   golden foliage
Blooms early autumn
Hardiness zone 6
Accent
Self sowing
Found in Italy to Albania
Height to 16 in. (40 cm)
Spreads 12 in. (30 cm)
Planting medium 6 in. (15 cm)
   deep
Full sun, mixed sun/shade

Not that attractive as an accent, but effective in mass, with golden fall color.

Sempervivum 'Saturn'

Sempervivum 'Silver Thaw'

Sesleria caerulea (Poaceae)
   White flowers, blue-green foliage
   Blooms midspring
   Hardiness zone 4
   Accent
   Self sowing
   Found in eastern Europe
   Height to 10 in. (25 cm)
   Spreads 12 in. (30 cm)
   Planting medium 6 in. (15 cm)
      deep
   Full sun, mixed sun/shade

Nice as an edge plant; used in mass plantings. Colorful foliage catches the eye.

Silene acaulis (Caryophyllaceae)
   Vivid pink flowers, green foliage
   Blooms late spring to early
      summer
   Hardiness zone 2

   Groundcover
   Not self sowing
   Found in mountains of central
      Europe, North America
   Height to 4 in. (10 cm)
   Spreads 10 in. (25 cm)
   Planting medium 6 in. (15 cm) deep
   Full sun

Extremely cold-hardy dwarf. Can be used on green roofs in northern US and at altitudes.

Sesleria autumnalis

Sesleria caerulea. Photograph by Georg Uebelhart, Jelitto Perennial Seeds.

Silene acaulis. Photograph by Georg Uebelhart, Jelitto Perennial Seeds.

Silene caroliniana subsp. wherryi (Caryophyllaceae)

Pink flowers, green foliage
Blooms late spring to midsummer
Hardiness zone 5
Groundcover
Not self sowing
Found in eastern and central North America
Height to 6 in. (15 cm)
Spreads 10 in. (25 cm)
Planting medium 6 in. (15 cm) deep
Full sun

Native of US East Coast. May not be long lived; needs additional water beyond rainfall.

Silene maritima 'Weisskehlchen' (Caryophyllaceae)

White flowers, green foliage
Blooms early to late summer
Hardiness zone 3
Groundcover
Not self sowing
Found in Atlantic coastal areas in US
Height to 8 in. (20 cm)
Spreads 12 in. (30 cm)
Planting medium 6 in. (15 cm) deep
Full sun

Very cold hardy. Will need reliable moisture, but delivers an attractive groundcover with a long bloom period.

Silene uniflora 'Compacta' (Caryophyllaceae)

Light pink flowers, green-gray foliage
Blooms early to late summer
Hardiness zone 3
Groundcover
Not self sowing
Found in Atlantic coastal areas in US
Height to 4 in. (10 cm)
Spreads 10 in. (25 cm)
Planting medium 6 in. (15 cm) deep
Full sun

Use in smaller scale plantings. Good mounding habit; interesting flower structure.

Silene caroliniana subsp. wherryi. Photograph by Georg Uebelhart, Jelitto Perennial Seeds.

Silene maritima 'Weisskehlchen'

Sporobolus heterolepis

(Poaceae)
Brown flowers, green foliage
Blooms midsummer to early
  autumn
Hardiness zone 6
Accent
Self sowing
Found in the US Great Plains, west
of the Mississippi River and east
of the Rockies
Height to 30 in. (76 cm)
Spreads 12 in. (30 cm)
Planting medium 6 in. (15 cm) deep
Full sun, mixed sun/shade

Graceful native grass. May need to mound medium before planting in drier locations.

Talinum calycinum (Portulacaceae)

Neon pink flowers, green foliage
Blooms midsummer to midautumn
Hardiness zone 6
Accent
Self sowing
Found in North America
Height to 4 in. (10 cm)
Spreads 2 in. (5 cm)
Planting medium 4 in. (10 cm) deep
Full sun

The showiest of the talinums, can be used as an annual in areas colder than its hardiness zone. Like all talinums, a favorite of honey bees, and foliage disappears at the first sign of frost.

Silene uniflora 'Compacta'

Sporobolus heterolepis. Photograph by Georg Uebelhart, Jelitto Perennial Seeds.

Talinum calycinum

Talinum paniculatum

(Portulacaceae)
Pink flowers, green foliage
Blooms midsummer to midautumn
Hardiness zone 8
Accent
Self sowing
Found in southern US to Central
    America
Height to 24 in. (60 cm)
Spreads 6 in. (15 cm)
Planting medium 4 in. (10 cm) deep
Full sun

Found throughout the Gulf Coast states in the US and used as a self-sowing annual in the northern US. Red flower pods add to its ornamental interest. Used as part of a showy display in front of the US Botanic Garden in Washington, D.C.

Talinum paniculatum

Talinum parviflorum

(Portulacaceae)
Light pink flowers, green foliage
Blooms midsummer to midautumn
Hardiness zone 6
Accent
Self sowing
Found in North America
Height to 8 in. (20 cm)
Spreads 4 in. (10 cm)
Planting medium 4 in. (10 cm) deep
Full sun

Found in the upper Great Plains, down to Arkansas and over to Arizona on rocky outcroppings. Suited for very dry and windy locations.

Talinum parviflorum

Talinum teretifolium

(Portulacaceae)
Rose-pink flowers, green foliage
Blooms midsummer to midautumn
Hardiness zone 6
Accent
Self sowing
Found from Pennsylvania down the
  Appalachians to Georgia
Height to 12 in. (30 cm)
Spreads 6 in. (15 cm)
Planting medium 4 in. (10 cm) deep
Full sun

Talinum teretifolium

On the threatened list throughout the mid-Atlantic region due to its shrinking habitat; green roofs present an opportunity for the plant's conservation.

Thymus citriodorus

(Lamiaceae)
Pale pink to lilac flowers, green-
  gold foliage
Blooms midsummer
Hardiness zone 5
Groundcover
Not self sowing
Found in temperate Europe and
  Asia
Height to 4 in. (10 cm)
Spreads 10 in. (25 cm)
Planting medium 6 in. (15 cm) deep
Full sun

Colorful foliage and lemony scent make this ideal for in between pavers and walkways. Needs additional water during a drought.

Thymus citriodorus

Thymus praecox 'Coccineus'
(Lamiaceae)
Rose-purple flowers, green foliage
Blooms midsummer
Hardiness zone 5
Groundcover
Not self sowing
Found in temperate Europe and
Asia
Height to 4 in. (10 cm)
Spreads 10 in. (25 cm)
Planting medium 6 in. (15 cm) deep
Full sun

Easy to find in the trade. Agreeable scent; suited for light foot traffic. Needs water to establish.

Thymus pulegioides (Lamiaceae)
Mauve flowers, green foliage
Blooms late spring to midautumn
Hardiness zone 5
Groundcover
Not self sowing
Found in temperate Europe and
Asia
Height to 4 in. (10 cm)
Spreads 10 in. (25 cm)
Planting medium 6 in. (15 cm) deep
Full sun

Strong bloomer, rapid groundcover. Like all thymes, can suffer in summer humidity.

Townsendia eximia
(Asteraceae)
White flowers with yellow centers,
green foliage
Blooms early summer
Hardiness zone 4
Accent
Self sowing
Found in western and southern
Central America
Height to 15 in. (38 cm)
Spreads 6 in. (15 cm)
Planting medium 4 in. (10 cm) deep
Full sun

Acts like an annual on a green roof; best on roofs in western US.

Thymus praecox 'Coccineus'

Thymus pulegioides

Triteleia ixioides (Alliaceae)

- Pale yellow flowers, green foliage
- Blooms late spring to late summer
- Hardiness zone 7
- Accent
- Self sowing
- Found in southwestern US to Oregon
- Height to 15 in. (38 cm)
- Spreads 8 in. (20 cm)
- Planting medium 6 in. (15 cm) deep
- Full sun

Allium-like plant that can be used at elevations to 5000 ft. (1524 m). Does not like shade; can tolerate some acidic conditions.

Tulbaghia violacea (Alliaceae)

- Purple flowers, green and white foliage
- Blooms midsummer
- Hardiness zone 7
- Accent
- Not self sowing
- Found in South Africa
- Height to 20 in. (50 cm)
- Spreads 6 in. (15 cm)
- Planting medium 4 in. (10 cm) deep
- Full sun

Also known as society garlic. Very ornamental and drought tolerant.

Townsendia eximia

Triteleia ixioides

Tulbaghia violacea

Veronica liwanensis

(Scrophulariaceae)
Blue flowers, green foliage
Blooms early spring to early summer
Hardiness zone 4
Groundcover
Not self sowing
Found in Caucasus mountains
Height to 2 in. (5 cm)
Spreads 8 in. (20 cm)
Planting medium 6 in. (15 cm) deep
Full sun, mixed sun/shade

Good in and around pavers and drains. Slowly makes a mat of small green leaves.

Veronica prostrata

(Scrophulariaceae)
Blue flowers, green foliage
Blooms late spring to early summer
Hardiness zone 5
Groundcover
Not self sowing
Found in Europe
Height to 4 in. (10 cm)
Spreads 10 in. (25 cm)
Planting medium 6 in. (15 cm) deep
Full sun, mixed sun/shade

Bigger, more showy flowers than the true carpet veronica. Will need reliable water.

Veronica repens

(Scrophulariaceae)
Pale blue flowers, green foliage
Blooms late spring to early summer
Hardiness zone 5
Groundcover
Not self sowing
Found in Spain and Corsica
Height to 2 in. (5 cm)
Spreads 10 in. (25 cm)
Planting medium 6 in. (15 cm) deep
Full sun, mixed sun/shade

Veronica liwanensis

Veronica prostrata. Photograph by Georg Uebelhart, Jelitto Perennial Seeds.

Can tolerate some foot traffic and can be used between pavers; needs irrigation.

Veronica whitleyi
  (Scrophulariaceae)
  Blue flowers, blue-green foliage
  Blooms late spring to midsummer
  Hardiness zone 3
  Groundcover
  Not self sowing
  Found in Europe
  Height to 2 in. (5 cm)
  Spreads 12 in. (30 cm)
  Planting medium 6 in. (15 cm) deep
  Full sun, mixed sun/shade

Soft foliage and a carpet of small flowers; semi-evergreen.

Veronica repens

Veronica whitleyi

Directory of Plants by Color and Type

THIS APPENDIX is intended to facilitate plant selection by flower color, foliage color, or plant type. This information should be especially useful for design professionals and others who consult this book on a regular basis.

Flower color

Blue flowers
Agastache rugosa
Aster oblongifolius
Campanula rotundifolia
Dracocephalum ruyschiana
Echium vulgare
Erigeron glaucus
Iris pumila
Lavandula angustifolia 'Hidcote Superior'
Linum perenne
Phacelia campanularia
Salvia pratensis
Scilla mischtschenkoana (syn. *S. tubergeniana*)
Veronica liwanensis
Veronica prostrata
Veronica repens
Veronica whitleyi

Brown flowers
Bouteloua curtipendula
Bouteloua gracilis
Buchloe dactyloides
Carex flacca
Carex humilis 'Hexe'
Deschampsia flexuosa

Linum flavum
Sesleria autumnalis
Sporobolus heterolepis

Green flowers
Poa alpina
Poa chaixii

Orange flowers
Agastache rupestris
Penstemon pinifolius
Pilosella aurantiaca (syn. *Hieracium aurantiacum*)

Pink flowers
Aethionema grandiflorum
Allium cernuum
Allium schoenoprasum
Allium senescens subsp. *montanum* var. *glaucum*
Antennaria dioica
Armeria maritima
Delosperma aberdeenense
Delosperma aberdeenense 'Abbey Rose'
Delosperma cooperi
Delosperma sutherlandii
Dianthus alpinus
Dianthus deltoides 'Brilliant'

Pink flowers (continued)
Dianthus myrtinervius
Goniolimon incanum
Kalanchoe thyrsiflora
Lychnis alpina
Petrorhagia saxifraga
Phlox subulata
Salvia jurisicii
Saponaria ocymoides
Scabiosa columbaria 'Misty
    Butterflies'
Sedum cauticola 'Lidakense'
Sedum ewersii
Sedum 'Matrona'
Sedum pluricaule 'Rosenteppich'
Sedum pluricaule var. *ezawe*
Sedum pulchellum
Sedum sieboldii
Sedum spurium 'Album
    Superbum',
Sedum spurium 'Fuldaglut'
Sedum spurium 'John Creech'
Sedum spurium 'Roseum'
Sedum spurium var. *album*
Sedum spurium 'Voodoo'
Sedum stoloniferum
Sempervivum arachnoideum
    'Sparkle'
Sempervivum 'Blue Boy'
Sempervivum 'Georgette'
Sempervivum 'Oddity'
Sempervivum 'Saturn'
Sempervivum 'Silver Thaw'
Silene acaulis
Silene caroliniana subsp. *wherryi*
Silene uniflora 'Compacta'
Talinum calycinum
Talinum paniculatum
Talinum parviflorum

Talinum teretifolium
Thymus citriodorus
Thymus praecox 'Coccineus'

Purple or violet flowers
Allium acuminatum
Allium oreophilum
Aster alpinus
Aster alpinus 'Dunkle Schöne'
Calluna vulgaris
Delosperma ecklonis var. *latifolia*
Delosperma 'Tiffendell Magenta'
Origanum vulgare
Penstemon smallii
Prunella grandiflora
Ruschia pulvinaris
Salvia officinalis
Salvia officinalis
Scutelleria alpina
Tulbaghia violacea

Red flowers
Aquilegia canadensis 'Little
    Lanterns'
Delosperma dyeri
Echium russicum
Malephora crocea var. *purpureo-*
    crocea 'Tequila Sunrise'
Sedum spurium 'Summer Glory'
Sedum telephium 'Emperor's
    Waves'

Silver flowers
Nassella tenuissima
Festuca idahoensis

White flowers
Achillea millefolium
Agastache rugosa f. *albiflora*
Allium tuberosum
Anacyclus pyrethrum var. *depressus*

Antennaria plantaginifolia

Arenaria montana

Armeria maritima 'Alba'

Cerastium tomentosum var. *columnae* 'Silberteppich'

Delosperma aberdeenense 'Abbey White'

Delosperma basuticum 'White Nugget'

Dianthus arenarius

Dianthus spiculifolius

Erigeron glaucus 'Albus'

Fragaria chiloensis

Herniaria glabra

Jovibarba 'Emerald Spring'

Marrubium incanum

Oenothera caespitosa

Orostachys aggregeatum

Orostachys boehmeri

Orostachys fimbriata

Rosularia chrysantha

Rosularia muratdaghensis

Salvia argentea

Sedum album

Sedum album 'Chloroticum'

Sedum album 'Coral Carpet'

Sedum album 'France'

Sedum album subsp. *teretifolium* 'Murale'

Sedum apoleipon

Sedum dasyphyllum

Sedum diffusum

Sedum hispanicum

Sedum moranense

Sedum pachyclados

Sedum stefco

Sedum telephioides

Sedum ternatum

Sesleria caerulea

Silene maritima 'Weisskehlchen'

Townsendia eximia

Yellow flowers

Achillea tomentosa

Alchemilla saxatilis

Allium moly

Alyssum montanum 'Berggold'

Alyssum serpyllifolium

Anthemis tinctoria

Anthyllis vulneraria

Artemisia ludoviciana

Artemisia stelleriana

Aurinia saxatilis 'Compacta' (syn. *Alyssum saxatile* 'Compactum')

Bulbine frutescens

Chrysopsis mariana

Crassula muscosa

Delosperma basuticum 'Gold Nugget'

Delosperma brunnthaleri

Delosperma nubigenum 'Basutoland'

Dianthus knappii

Erigeron linearis

Eriogonum flavum

Eriophyllum lanatum

Euphorbia myrsinites

Galium verum

Hieracium alpinum

Hieracium lanatum

Hieracium spilophaeum 'Leopard'

Hieracium villosum

Lotus corniculatus

Malephora lutea

Oenothera macrocarpa (syn. *O. missouriensis*)

Oenothera macrocarpa subsp. *incana*

Yellow flowers (continued)

Opuntia humifusa (syn. *O. compressa*)

Othonna capensis

Pilosella officinarum (syn. *Hieracium pilosella*)

Potentilla aurea

Potentilla crantzii

Potentilla neumanniana (syn. *P. verna*)

Santolina rosmarinifolia

Scutellaria alpina 'Moonbeam'

Sedum acre 'Aureum'

Sedum acre 'Oktoberfest'

Sedum aizoon 'Euphorbioides'

Sedum divergens

Sedum forsterianum subsp. *elegans*

Sedum 'Green Spruce'

Sedum griseum

Sedum hybridum 'Czar's Gold'

Sedum hybridum 'Immergrünchen'

Sedum kamtschaticum

Sedum kamtschaticum var. *floriferum* 'Weihenstephaner Gold'

Sedum kamtschaticum var. *kamtschaticum* 'Variegatum'

Sedum lanceolatum

Sedum lineare 'Variegatum'

Sedum lydium

Sedum makinoi

Sedum mexicanum

Sedum middendorffianum var. *diffusum*

Sedum ochroleucum

Sedum oreganum

Sedum ×rubrotinctum

Sedum ×rubrotinctum (dwarf form)

Sedum rupestre (syn. *S. reflexum*)

Sedum rupestre 'Angelina'

Sedum sarmentosum

Sedum sediforme

Sedum selskianum

Sedum sexangulare

Sedum sichotense

Sedum spathulifolium

Sedum stahlii

Sedum stenopetalum

Sedum tetractinum

Sedum urvillei

Triteleia ixioides

Foliage color

Blue foliage

Sedum 'Bertram Anderson'

Sedum cauticola 'Lidakense'

Sedum dasyphyllum

Sedum griseum

Sedum hispanicum

Sedum ochroleucum

Sedum rupestre (syn. *S. reflexum*)

Sedum rupestre 'Angelina'

Sedum sediforme

Sedum urvillei

Sesleria caerulea

Blue-green foliage

Agastache rupestris

Allium senescens subsp. *montanum* var. *glaucum*

Bouteloua curtipendula

Koeleria glauca

Othonna capensis

Sedum ewersii

Sedum pachyclados

Sedum pluricaule 'Rosenteppich'

Sempervivum 'Blue Boy'

Veronica whitleyi

Gray foliage

Antennaria dioica
Artemisia ludoviciana
Artemisia stelleriana
Cerastium tomentosum var. *columnae* 'Silberteppich'
Kalanchoe thyrsiflora
Lavandula angustifolia 'Hidcote Superior'
Oenothera macrocarpa subsp. *incana*
Orostachys boehmeri
Poa alpina
Rosularia muratdaghensis
Salvia officinalis
Santolina rosmarinifolia
Sedum ×rubrotinctum
Sedum spathulifolium

Green and red foliage

Jovibarba 'Emerald Spring'
Sempervivum 'Georgette'
Sempervivum 'Saturn'

Green and white foliage

Sedum kamtschaticum var. *kamtschaticum* 'Variegatum'
Tulbaghia violacea

Purple foliage

Sedum pluricaule var. *ezawe*
Sedum telephium 'Emperor's Waves'

Silver foliage

Pilosella officinarum (syn. *Hieracium pilosella*)
Salvia argentea
Sempervivum 'Silver Thaw'

Yellow-green foliage

Rosularia chrysantha
Sempervivum arachnoideum 'Sparkle'
Thymus citriodorus

Plant type

Grasses

Buchloe dactyloides
Carex flacca
Carex humilis 'Hexe'
Deschampsia flexuosa
Festuca idahoensis
Koeleria glauca
Koeleria macrantha (syn. *K. pyramidata*)
Nassella tenuissima
Poa alpina
Poa chaixii
Sesleria autumnalis
Sesleria caerulea
Sporobolus heterolepis

North American natives

Agastache rupestris
Allium cernuum
Aquilegia canadensis 'Little Lanterns'
Artemisia ludoviciana
Aster oblongifolius
Bouteloua curtipendula
Bouteloua gracilis
Buchloe dactyloides
Chrysopsis mariana
Deschampsia flexuosa
Erigeron glaucus
Erigeron glaucus 'Albus'
Erigeron linearis
Eriogonum flavum

North American natives
(continued)

Eriophyllum lanatum
Fragaria chiloensis
Linum perenne
Oenothera caespitosa
Oenothera macrocarpa (syn. *O. missouriensis*)
Opuntia humifusa (syn. *O. compressa*)
Penstemon pinifolius
Penstemon smallii
Phacelia campanularia
Phlox subulata
Sedum divergens
Sedum lanceolatum
Sedum oreganum
Sedum pulchellum
Sedum stenopetalum
Sedum telephioides
Sedum ternatum
Silene caroliniana subsp. *wherryi*
Silene maritima 'Weisskehlchen'
Silene uniflora 'Compacta'
Sporobolus heterolepis
Talinum calycinum
Talinum paniculatum
Talinum parviflorum
Talinum teretifolium
Townsendia eximia
Triteleia ixioides

Herbs

Allium schoenoprasum
Allium tuberosum
Lavandula angustifolia 'Hidcote Superior'
Marrubium incanum
Origanum vulgare
Prunella grandiflora
Salvia officinalis
Thymus citriodorus
Thymus praecox 'Coccineus'
Thymus pulegioides

Self sowers

Achillea millefolium
Achillea tomentosa
Allium acuminatum
Allium cernuum
Allium moly
Allium oreophilum
Allium schoenoprasum
Allium senescens subsp. *montanum* var. *glaucum*
Allium tuberosum
Anthemis tinctoria
Aquilegia canadensis 'Little Lanterns'
Bouteloua curtipendula
Bouteloua gracilis
Buchloe dactyloides
Deschampsia flexuosa
Euphorbia myrsinites
Festuca idahoensis
Hieracium alpinum
Hieracium lanatum
Hieracium spilophaeum 'Leopard'
Hieracium villosum
Nassella tenuissima
Oenothera caespitosa
Oenothera macrocarpa (syn. *O. missouriensis*)
Papaver alpinum hybrids
Petrorhagia saxifraga
Phacelia campanularia
Pilosella aurantiaca (syn. *Hieracium aurantiacum*)

Pilosella officinarum (syn. *Hieracium pilosella*)
Sedum pulchellum
Sesleria autumnalis
Sesleria caerulea
Sporobolus heterolepis

Talinum calycinum
Talinum paniculatum
Talinum parviflorum
Talinum teretifolium
Townsendia eximia
Triteleia ixioides

Seed and Plant Nurseries

Bluebird Nursery, Inc.
P.O. Box 460
Clarkson, NE 68629
800.356.9164
www.bluebirdnursery.com

Emory Knoll Farms
3410 Ady Road
Street, MD 21154
410.452.5880
www.greenroofplants.com

Hortech
P.O. Box 533
Spring Lake, MI 49456
616.842.1392
www.premiumplants.net

Intrinsic Perennial Gardens
10702 Seaman Road
Hebron, IL 60034
815.648.2788
www.intrinsicperennialgardens.com

Jelitto Perennial Seeds
125 Chenoweth Lane
Suite 301
Louisville, KY 40207
502.895.0807
www.jelitto.com

Jost Greenhouses
12348 Eckelmann Lane
St. Louis, MO 63131
314. 821.2834
www.jostgreenhouses.com

Little Hill Nursery
5494 Raleigh LaGrange Road
Memphis, TN 38134
901.246.1314

NATS Nursery, Ltd.
24555 32nd Avenue
Langley, B.C.
Canada V2Z 2J5
604.530.9300
www.natsnursery.com

North Creek Nurseries, Inc.
388 North Creek Road
Landenberg, PA 19350
877.326.7584
www.northcreeknurseries.com

Rana Creek
35351 East Carmel Valley Road
Carmel Valley, CA 93924
831.659.3820
www.ranacreek.com

Saul Nurseries
1115 West Nancy Creek Drive
Atlanta, GA 30319
404. 257.3339
www.saulnurseries.com

Bibliography

Arbeitskreis Fassadenbegrünung. 2000. *Richtlinie für die Planung, Ausführung und Pflege von Fassadenbegrünung mit Kletterpflanzen.* Bonn, Germany: Forschungsgesellschaft Landschaftsentwicklung Landschaftsbau (FLL).

Beattie, D. 2003. Native and ornamental plant survival research. In *Greening Rooftops for Sustainable Communities, Proceedings of the First North American Green Roofs Conference, Chicago, May 2003.* Toronto: The Cardinal Group.

———. 2005. Interview with author, 28 June.

Beattie, D., and R. Berghage. 2004. Green roof media characteristics: the basics. In *Greening Rooftops for Sustainable Communities, Proceedings of the Second North American Green Roofs Conference, Portland, June 2004.* Toronto: The Cardinal Group.

Berghage, R. 2005. Personal correspondence with author, 2 August.

Brenneisen, S. 2003. The benefits of biodiversity from green roofs: key design consequences. In *Greening Rooftops for Sustainable Communities, Proceedings of the First North American Green Roofs Conference, Chicago, May 2003.* Toronto: The Cardinal Group.

Breuning, J. 2005a. Personal correspondence with author, 14 April.

———. 2005b. Interview with author, 3 May.

Bundesverband Garten-, Landschafts- und Sportplatzbau e.V. 2002. *Jahrbuch Dachbegrünung 2002.* Braunschweig, Germany: Bernhard Thalacker Verlag.

Cave, Y. 2003. *Succulents for the contemporary garden.* Portland, Oregon: Timber Press.

Cheney, C. 2002. Greening Gotham's rooftops. *Green Roofs Infrastructure Monitor,* 4(2).

Dörries, J., and U. Zens. 2003. Multifunktionale Dachvegetation. *Garten + Landschaft* (October): 22–25.

Drupka, B. 1992. *Dachbegrünung: Pflanzen- und Vegetationsanwendung an Bauwerken.* Stuttgart: Ulmer.

Dunnett, N. 2002. Up on the roof. *The Garden* (May): 380–383.

Dunnett, N., and N. Kingsbury. 2004a. *Planting Green Roofs and Living Walls*. Portland, Oregon: Timber Press.

————. 2004b. Planting options for extensive and semi-extensive green roofs. In *Greening Rooftops for Sustainable Communities, Proceedings of the Second North American Green Roofs Conference, Portland, June 2004*. Toronto: The Cardinal Group.

Earth Justice. 2004. Sewage discharges in Washington DC waterways. http://www.earthjustice.org/urgent/display. Accessed 4 February 2005.

Earth Pledge. 2005. *Green Roofs: Ecological Design and Construction*. Atglen, Pennsylvania: Schiffer Publishing Ltd.

Eggli, U., ed. 2003. *Illustrated Handbook of Succulent Plants: Crassulaceae*. Berlin: Springer.

Elvidge, C., C. Milesi, J. Dietz, B. Tuttle, P. Sutton, R. Nemani, and J. Vogelmann. 2004. U.S. constructed area approaches the size of Ohio. *Eos* 85 (24): 233–240.

Emilsson, T. 2003. The influence of establishment method and species mix on plant cover. In *Greening Rooftops for Sustainable Communities, Proceedings of the First North American Green Roofs Conference, Chicago, May 2003*. Toronto: The Cardinal Group.

Forschungsgesellschaft Landschaftsentwicklung Landschaftsbau e.V. 2002. *Guideline for the Planning, Execution and Upkeep of Green-Roof Sites*. Bonn: Forschungsgesellschaft Landschaftsentwicklung Landschaftsbau e.V.

Gaulin, M. 2005. Personal correspondence with author, 12 August.

Gedge, D. 2003. From rubble to redstarts. In *Greening Rooftops for Sustainable Communities, Proceedings of the First North American Green Roofs Conference, Chicago, May 2003*. Toronto: The Cardinal Group.

Green Roofs for Healthy Cities. 2004. Participant manual for Green Roof Design 101, Introductory Course. Toronto: The Cardinal Group.

Griffiths, M. 1994. *The New Royal Horticultural Society Dictionary: Index of Garden Plants*. London: Macmillan Press.

Hauth, E., and T. Liptan. 2003. Plant survival findings in the Pacific Northwest. In *Greening Rooftops for Sustainable Communities, Proceedings of the First North American Green Roofs Conference, Chicago, May 2003*. Toronto: The Cardinal Group.

Herman, R. 2003. Green roofs in Germany: Yesterday, today and tomorrow. In *Greening Rooftops for Sustainable Communities, Proceedings of the First North American Green Roofs Conference, Chicago, May 2003*. Toronto: The Cardinal Group.

Hunt, W. 2005. Telephone interview with author, 1 July.

Hutchinson, D., P. Abrams, R. Retzlaff, and T. Liptan. 2003. Stormwater monitoring of two ecoroofs in Portland, Oregon, USA. In *Greening Rooftops for Sustainable Communities, Proceedings of the First North American Green Roofs Conference, Chicago, May 2003*. Toronto: The Cardinal Group.

Jelitto, L., and W. Schacht. 1990. *Hardy Herbaceous Perennials*. 2 vols. Portland: Timber Press.

Jelitto Staudensamen. 2005. Catalogue. Schwarmstedt, Germany: Jelitto Staudensamen GmbH.

Johnson, J., and J. Newton. 1993. *Building Green: A Guide to Using Plants on Roofs, Walls and Pavements*. London: London Ecology Unit.

Kats, G. 2004. Are green buildings cost-effective? *Green@work* magazine. http:www.greenatworkmag.com. Accessed 14 April 2005.

———. 2005. Telephone interview with author, 3 May.

Kiers, A. 2002. *Greenroofs: The Last Urban Frontier*. Master's Thesis, University of California, Berkeley.

Kolb, W., and T. Schwarz. 1999. *Dachbegrünung intensiv und extensiv*. Stuttgart: Ulmer.

LaBerge, K., K. Worthington, P. Mulvaney, and R. Bolliger. 2005. City of Chicago green roof test plot study: stormwater and temperature results. In *Greening Rooftops for Sustainable Communities, Proceedings of the Third North American Green Roofs Conference, Washington, D.C., May 2005*. Toronto: The Cardinal Group.

Livingston, E. H., C. Miller, and M. Lohr. 2004. Green roof design and implementation in Florida. In *Greening Rooftops for Sustainable Communities, Proceedings of the Second North American Green Roofs Conference, Portland, June 2004*. Toronto: The Cardinal Group.

McGary, J., ed. 2003. *Rock Garden Design and Construction by the North American Rock Garden Society*. Portland, Oregon: Timber Press.

Miller, C. 2003. Moisture management in green roofs. In *Greening Rooftops for Sustainable Communities, Proceedings of the First North American Green Roofs Conference, Chicago, May 2003*. Toronto: The Cardinal Group.

———. 2004. Performance-based approach to preparing green roof specifications. In *Greening Rooftops for Sustainable Communities, Proceedings of the Second North American Green Roofs Conference, Portland, June 2004*. Toronto: The Cardinal Group.

———. 2005. Personal correspondence with author, 7 and 15 July.

Monterusso, M., D. B. Rowe, and C. Rugh. 2005. Establishment and persistence of *Sedum* spp. and native taxa for green roof applications. *HortScience* 40 (2): 391–396.

Moran, A., W. Hunt, and G. Jennings. 2004. A North Carolina field study to evaluate greenroof runoff quantity, runoff quality, and plant growth. In *Greening Rooftops for Sustainable Communities, Proceedings of the Second North American Green Roofs Conference, Portland, June 2004.* Toronto: The Cardinal Group.

Moran, A., W. Hunt, and J. Smith. 2005. Hydrologic and water quality performance from greenroofs in Goldsboro and Raleigh, North Carolina. In *Greening Rooftops for Sustainable Communities, Proceedings of the Third North American Green Roofs Conference, Washington, D.C., May 2005.* Toronto: The Cardinal Group.

New York Climate and Health Project. 2004. Assessing potential public health and air quality impacts of changing climate and land use in metropolitan New York. New York: Columbia University. http://www. earthinstitute.columbia.edu/events/2004/images/NYCHP_Briefing_ Paper_June04.pdf. Accessed 16 April 2005.

Ohlwein, K. 1984. Dachbegrünung: ökologisch und funtionsgerecht. Wiesbaden: Bauverlag.

Optigrün. 2005. Catalogue. Krauchenwies-Göggingen, Germany: Optigrün international AG.

Osmundson, T. 1999. *Roof Gardens, History, Design, Construction.* New York: W. W. Norton and Co.

Peck, S. 2005. Telephone interview with author, 22 April.

Pomerantz, M., H. Akbari, P. Berdahl, H. G. Taha, and A. H. Rosenfeld. 1999. Physics and public policy for urban heat island mitigation. Paper presented at American Physical Society Conference, March 1999, in Atlanta, Georgia.

Rowe, B., R. Clayton, N. Van Woert, M. Monterusso, and D. Russell. 2003. The influence of green roof slope, substrate depth and vegetation on runoff. In *Greening Rooftops for Sustainable Communities, Proceedings of the First North American Green Roofs Conference, Chicago, May 2003.* Toronto: The Cardinal Group.

Rowe, B., M. Monterusso, and R. Clayton. 2005. Evaluation of *Sedum* species and Michigan native taxa for green roof applications. In *Greening Rooftops for Sustainable Communities, Proceedings of the Third North American Green Roofs Conference, Washington, D.C., May 2005.* Toronto: The Cardinal Group.

Rowe, B. 2005. Personal correspondence with author, 20 July.

Smith, G., P. Chesselet, E. van Jaarsveld, H. Hartmann, S. Hammer, B. van Wyk, P. Burgoyne, C. Klak, and H. Kurzweil. 1998. *Mesembs of the World: Illustrated Guide to a Remarkable Succulent Group*. Pretoria: Briza Publications.

Snodgrass, E. 2005. 100 extensive green roofs: lessons learned. In *Greening Rooftops for Sustainable Communities, Proceedings of the Third North American Green Roofs Conference, Washington, D.C., May 2005*. Toronto: The Cardinal Group.

Staff of the L. H. Bailey Hortorium, Cornell University. 1976. *Hortus Third: A Concise Dictionary of Plants Cultivated in the United States and Canada*. 2 vols. New York: Wiley.

Stephenson, R. 1994. *Sedum: Cultivated Stonecrops*. Portland, Oregon: Timber Press.

Thuring, C. E. 2005. *Green Roof Plant Responses to Different Media and Depths When Exposed to Drought*. Master's Thesis, Pennsylvania State University.

Todd, N. J., and J. Todd. 1993. *From Eco-Cities to Living Machines: Principles of Ecological Design*. Berkeley, California: North Atlantic Books.

Van Woert, N., D. B Rowe, J. A. Andresen, C. L. Rugh, and L. Xiao. 2005[a]. Watering regime and green roof substrate design affect *Sedum* plant growth. *HortScience* 40 (3): 1–6.

Van Woert, N., D. B. Rowe, J. A. Andresen, C. L. Rugh, R. T. Fernandez, and L. Xiao. 2005b. Green roof stormwater retention: effects of roof surface, slope, and media depth. *Journal of Environmental Quality* 34: 1036–1044.

White, J. W. 2001. Green roof infrastructure & preventing fire hazards. *Green Roofs Infrastructure Monitor* 3 (1): 9.

———. 2005a. Extensive greenroof plant characteristics and selection. Paper presented at EPA Green Roofscaping Conference, 7 April 2005, Denver, Colorado.

———. 2005b. Interviews with author in Durango, Colorado, 25 May, and personal correspondence, 6 May, 9 June, 2 July, and 5 July.

White J. W., and E. Snodgrass. 2003. Extensive green roof plant selection and characteristics. In *Greening Rooftops for Sustainable Communities, Proceedings of the First North American Green Roofs Conference, Chicago, May 2003*. Toronto: The Cardinal Group.

Index

Illustrations appear on page numbers shown in *italic*.